B.C.

DOCUMENTS OF MODERN HISTORY

General Editors:

A. G. Dickens
Director, Institute of Historical Research, University of London

Alun Davies
Professor of Modern History, University College of Swansea

VICTORIAN
NONCONFORMITY

edited by

John Briggs

Lecturer in History,
University of Keele

and

Ian Sellers

Padgate College of Education,
Warrington

Edward Arnold

First published 1973 by
Edward Arnold (Publishers) Ltd.,
25 Hill Street, London W1X 8LL

Clothbound edition ISBN: 0 7131 5728 3
Paper edition ISBN: 0 7131 5729 1

Printed in Great Britain by
Butler & Tanner Ltd., Frome and London

CONTENTS

INTRODUCTION

'If the Jesuit,' writes Miss Margaret Maison, 'was only too often a nasty piece of work in Victorian fiction, so also was the Dissenter. But whereas the Jesuit and his intrigues were at least clever, exotic and exciting, the Dissenter was usually shown as ignorant, drab, provincial and depressing.'[1] Whether it be in Dickens or Mrs Oliphant, Mark Rutherford or Charlotte Bronte, Mrs Humphrey Ward or Arnold Bennett the type is not a very flattering one. But neither the caricatures of the novels nor the open censures of that rather superior person Matthew Arnold should be allowed too hastily to dismiss the Nonconformists from the Victorian scene. The adjectives 'ignorant, drab, provincial and depressing' are far from expressing the whole truth about them. Contrast Lord John Russell's judgment: 'I know the Dissenters, they carried the Reform Bill; they carried the abolition of slavery; they carried Free Trade; and they'll carry the abolition of Church Rates.'[2] The Nonconformists championed those movements and sentiments whch may be considered most characteristically Victorian: indeed theirs was a crucial contribution to the making of Victorian England.

Three generations and a diversity of denominational traditions ensure that any brief survey of Victorian nonconformity will be open to the charge of neglecting themes which some might feel crucial to the telling of the story. The editors of the present volume would, in defence of their selection, argue that they have tried to illustrate that which was central and normative. Rather than illustrate the development of the several denominations they have tried to present the feel of those things which concerned Nonconformists as a whole: similarly they have not attempted to illustrate the regional developments of Dissent though they have been concerned to ensure that the voice of provincial Dissent is not drowned by the sonorous declamations of the church bureaucrats and the princes of the metropolitan pulpit. One further limitation has been the constraint of limiting the illustrations to words without recourse to architecture and paintings, old

[1] M. Maison, *Search Your Soul Eustace* (1961), p. 183.
[2] Cited by E. A. Payne, *The Free Church Tradition in the Life of England* (2nd edn., 1965), p. 101.

class tickets and celebration china, tracts in their original printed form, not to mention the irreverent comments of the cartoonist. It is not, for example, without significance that whilst Methodist Staffordshire produced a rostrum full of Nonconformist divines, preachers, and evangelists in folk pottery, and added to their number half a dozen eminent Roman Catholics, there is no evidence of the manufacture of a figure of any Anglican priest or prelate. Nevertheless, included in the present selection is as diverse a collection of types of source material as the printed page allows: press comment, diary and minute book, fiction and poetry, hymns and sermons.

The young Arthur Porritt's first assignment as a reporter for the *Manchester Examiner* in 1890 was to attend the Metropolitan Tabernacle. His instructions were: 'If Spurgeon preaches just a gospel sermon, there is no copy in it. If he says anything about himself that may make a good paragraph; if he says anything about current questions give us it in full.'[3] Concern for those gospel sermons is just that quality which distinguishes the historian from the journalist, for it is they which, useless for copy, explain the adherence to Spurgeon of so large a congregation over so many years, for the sermon was the focus of Nonconformist life in the nineteenth century, at once at the centre of the week's liturgy, the all-important imperative demanding response in practical Christianity, the educator of conscience, mind and feelings. In consequence it would be foolish to attempt an understanding of the behaviour of the Nonconformists without regard for what the men of the times declared to be their crucial diet of instruction, stimulation and assurance.

The religion of the Nonconformists as proclaimed in these sermons can be usefully considered as a compound of three different historical processes, overlapping yet distinct. The first ingredient was seventeenth-century Puritanism with its emphasis upon order, law and authority (though the nature of that order, law and authority was different according to whether the tradition sprang from high Genevan orthodoxy or whether, as was the case with the Quakers, Unitarians and some Baptists, inspiration came from more radical sources).

Secondly, the select religion of the Puritans had for many Nonconformists been qualified by the ardour, vitality, and enthusiasm of eighteenth-century Evangelicalism with its concern for experience rather than argument. Thus whilst the Evangelical Revival re-invigorated the sadly moribund dissenting congregations of the middle of the eighteenth century it also changed the flavour of their church-life. John Marlowe perhaps only indulges in a pardonable overstatement

[3] A. Porritt, *The Best I Remember* (1922), p. 1.

when he suggests 'Puritanism tended to repel people by the ease with which one was damned, Methodism by the ease with which one could be saved'.[4]

The interaction of these two forces is critical: thus Dr Nuttall asserts, 'It was during the eighteenth century that historic Dissent took the form in which it has been a recognizable part of the English scene; and the poles between which, by attraction or repulsion, it did so, were Calvinism and the Evangelical Revival', and illustrates the ambivalence of some who would be accounted 'moderate Calvinists' with respect to these reference points by citing the obituary of one, Nathanael Trotman (d. 1793): 'His sentiments were strictly Calvinistic; his subjects purely evangelical. In his preaching there was the light of doctrine, without the dryness of system; the warmth of experience without the wild-fire of enthusiasm, the necessity of morality without the ostentation of pharisaism'[5]—in other words Trotman was able to encompass the virtues of Calvinism and Evangelicalism, the 'light of doctrine' and the 'warmth of experience' without their pathological excesses, the 'dryness of system' and the 'wild-fire of enthusiasm'.

In theology, therefore, Nonconformity represented a spectrum of beliefs from the Evangelical Arminianism of the Methodists through the moderate Calvinism of the majority to some whose essential Puritanism was little affected by the movements of the previous century: for the most part there was much common ground—only the Unitarians, representing the rationalism of the left, and the hyper-Calvinists representing the rationalism of the right self-consciously inhabited the peripheries of dissent. From another viewpoint, it was the Wesleyans, with their submission to connexionalism and their Tory politics who were the odd ones out: if in the eighteenth century the Wesleyans had had slowly to learn the impossibility of existence as a society within the Church of England, it took the whole of the nineteenth century for them to reconcile themselves to the fraternity of dissent, and all the persuasion of Hugh Price Hughes to wean them away from Toryism and to encourage their active and eager participation in the Free Church movement at the end of the century. Even though the Free Church movement, with its unhesitating advocacy of simultaneous evangelism, clearly stood within the Evangelical tradition, a powerful High-Church Wesleyan group held aloof from its activities, still unpersuaded of the Nonconformist character of Methodism.

[4] J. Marlowe, *The Puritan Tradition* (1956), p. 45.
[5] G. Nuttall, 'Calvinism in Free Church History' in *The Baptist Quarterly*, XXII, No. 8, October 1968, p. 420.

Nineteenth-century Nonconformity is, however, more than a compound of Puritanism and Evangelicalism—both these had been tempered by the experience of social exclusion, the consciousness of which became heightened in the context of the suspicions of the 1790s to lead on to the campaigns of 'Political Dissent' in the early nineteenth century with its ever-increasing appetite for further instalments of equality with every concession won.

The struggle between church and chapel represented two different worlds engaged in uncomprehending battle the one with the other: it was not simply a question of 'the chapels of the industrial revolution confronting the churches of the rural squirearchy';[6] urban Anglicanism and rural dissent were equally part of the conflict. It was a contest between an ecclesiastical order at once established and episcopal and the several federations of nonconforming churches, more or less tightly organized, whose transient survival depended upon their capacity to collect a congregation and serve a contemporary need. The early years of the nineteenth century witness their considerable success in both these directions and it was this success that bred both their antipathy to the Church of England and their appetites for equal rights in what was necessarily becoming a pluralist state.

It was the Dissenters' disabilities, in fact, which were parents to that process whereby Victorian Nonconformists for all their latent pietism, were enticed into the besmirched world of politics in general, and into alliance with the Liberal Party in particular. This was the process that Edward Miall harnessed all too successfully in his attempt to identify the interests of Nonconformity with those of the Liberation Society.

Guiness Rogers saw the Anti-Corn Law League campaign as seminal in this process: 'it was really a starting point in the public life of the Free Churches', because for the first time 'in English history the voice of nonconformist ministers was heard in such strength upon affairs which seemed to lie outside their proper province'.[7] The issue was a significant one, for it indicated how far large sections of Nonconformity were prepared to adopt a laissez-faire attitude to the state, to argue that the best society was that which was least coerced, where government activity was restrained as much as possible. Involvement in politics may have originated in a selfish concern to secure justice for one's own: it was soon realized that herein also lay responsibility, the

[6] David Martin, *A Sociology of English Religion* (1967), p. 18.
[7] J. G. Rogers, *An Autobiography* (1903), p. 80.

responsibility of submitting politics to Christian principles, not in general terms but with uncomfortable precision. Dale heavily censured those ministers who, whilst willing to see the hand of God in national disasters, and to call their people to consequent repentance, 'yet think that there is something like profanation in attempting to show from the pulpit by what particular measures our legislation might be made more righteous and Christian'. Indeed, he could look back wistfully from the nineties after the split in the Liberal Party and confess that twenty years earlier 'the Liberal party in Birmingham, was in many respects like a secular Church'.[8] This relationship between pietism and political involvement is crucial to an understanding of Victorian Nonconformity: some gave themselves to either the one or the other, but perhaps most characteristic were those who held the two together in uneasy tension. So, for example, the Nonconformist conscience worked to the rule that politics and personalities can never be separated: corrupt politicians are incapable of producing good policies, a principle which though it worked against the Liberal Party in the person of Parnell, also brought it mammoth support through the mediation of Mr Gladstone, 'one of the very few statesmen who feel that the law of Christ is to govern nations as well as individuals'.[9]

The Liberation Society and the Liberal Party, in the context of the disintegration of the Calvinist synthesis, all too easily conspired to fill the theological vacuum with brash forms of religious activism. Contradictions abounded: on the one hand faith was defined exclusively in personal terms and every form of ecclesiastical organization that went beyond the solitary saint was easily discounted by the attachment of the label 'institutional'. Yet at the same time all manner of societies were established following purely secular patterns for the discharge of the different responsibilities increasingly felt by the Christian conscience. Amidst this welter of activity the concept of the church was increasingly confused and altered so that the old Puritan concept of the covenant community gives way to the reality of a Christian presence represented by a range of Christian societies engaged in various aspects of the great missionary task, a task, it should be noted, that pre-Evangelical Dissent had fatally spurned. The broader interests of the later nineteenth century did not fundamentally alter the model—the only difference being that the many auxiliaries were concerned to proffer a social gospel instead of a dogmatic one. The organic view of the church with

[8] A. W. W. Dale, *Life of R. W. Dale* (1898), pp. 250–51, 634–5.
[9] Guiness Rogers in *The Congregationalist*, October 1879, p. 862.

its stress upon mutual responsibility within the Christian commonwealth was replaced by a streamlined machine, powerfully tooled up for Evangelism and social redemption—and sometimes, it must be confessed not even that, for large urban congregations, gathered together in great solid temples of middle-class respectability, possessed neither the common life of the meeting house nor the urgent concern to pursue the lost and the needy of the nineteenth-century religious societies, but existed rather by some kind of self-justifying principle in themselves. Well might a correspondent to the *Patriot* complain that a church of over a thousand seats was a betrayal of Nonconformist principles.

Victorian Nonconformists had little time for creeds and articles, particularly since these had been used as a discipline to secure their exclusion not merely from the church from which they had willingly separated but also from the state, full membership of which they so much desired. Further, their knowledge of the eighteenth century taught them that the most rigorous articles and confessions were manifestly impotent to guard the orthodoxy of the church, let alone its spiritual life. Concern for spirituality had by the early nineteenth century been dogmatized as 'non-credalism': an ugly word representing that reluctance to define doctrine which though prevalent amongst Victorian Nonconformists was not altogether shared by either seventeenth-century Puritan or eighteenth-century Evangelical. It was not of course about belief that they were agnostic, but about the capacity of language to confine belief in words and to express spiritual truth—'assent to abstract propositions however true is not Christian faith', affirmed the *Eclectic Review* for 1851. In the context of the break-up of the Calvinist synthesis and of the challenge of new knowledge, 'non-credalism', though never intended to do so, made both for greater flexibility in doctrine, an easier accommodation of new thought and for greater difficulty in defining and discerning heresy. The impact of these processes of mind represents a formidable change in belief, practice and ethos. In one sense 'non-credalism' at the beginning of the century meant very little, for there was then, denominational differences notwithstanding, a remarkable homogeneity about Nonconformist theology: when the adjective evangelical was added it did little more than exclude the increasingly peripheral Unitarians and a few fellow-travellers in the orthodox denominations. By the end of the century this cohesion is gone: over against evangelical Nonconformists there are now 'broad-church Nonconformists' and even rumours of a 'high church Dissent', whilst in relation to the Bible a whole spectrum of attitudes from antique literalism to the most corrosive modernism was to be found. The implications of the new intellectual climate were very wide: biological science appeared to be attacking not only the reliability of the Biblical record but also the Christian doctrine of man; in a mechanistic universe the function of prayer became uncertain; could prayer in fact be reconciled with the universal rule of scientific law? Hell, which had occupied the attention of so many Nonconformist Brimstones, now seemed more remote and less certainly populated than it had once been. When entrenched conservatism encountered foot-loose liberalism on all these issues, it was little wonder that the tradition of 'non-credalism' came under scrutiny. It gave the liberal all the freedom he wanted whilst the old-fashioned Dissenter continued a traditional hostility to creeds. Both had now, however, to defend this position against the pleas for a neo-credalism that Conservatives like Spurgeon were anxious to secure. When on behalf of neo-credalism he threw down the gauntlet to the Baptist churches in the Downgrade Controversy of 1888, the Baptist Union, though urged by many to have nothing to do with doctrinal definitions, concluded the dispute by agreeing a 'Declaratory Statement', which though accused of representing a mere lowest common denominator of theological commitment, in fact bore family resemblance to the doctrinal basis of the Evangelical Alliance of 1846.

These problems of belief were serious enough but the hazards of the moment were magnified by the increasing consciousness that Non-conformity was becoming more and more a middle-class phenomenon; in other words that it needed not only an intellectual but a social justification. But each of these demands seemed to prejudice the success of the other, for the intellectually defensible faith seemed to be too sophisticated to be socially commendable. As early as 1850 the Reverend T. Adkins told the Congregational Union that the danger was that the churches in their battle with rationalism would overlook the needs of the religion-less classes of industrial England: there had been much argument, perhaps too much, but the real need was for much mission. It was not a new scholasticism but a new determination to make disciples that was required of the church: alarm at the danger to the faith implicit in 'pantheistic speculation' and 'bewildered criticism' was appropriate but the real danger of the impact of 'Teutonic' philosophy was that it was taking place when the Christian faith was unknown to many Englishmen. The situation was a cruel one: the intellectual situation demanded greater mental vigour of the clergy to meet the charges and claims of the critics, but the social situation demanded simple and uncomplicated preaching to vast unchurched masses whose traditional unbelief might be fortified by what they took to be the implications of scientific discovery, though they could not follow the subtle technicalities argued by theological apologists in defending orthodox belief.

There were, of course, other reasons for increasing working-class estrangement—principally, of course, the social pretensions acquired by those chapel communities which were feeling the impact of new prosperity. With the development at the end of the century of more single-class suburbs, single-class churches emerged, a particularly hazardous development for those denominations that believed in the autonomy of the local church. The down-town church—in its heyday often something of a Gothic status-symbol—was now left as an expensive relic to a congregation depleted numerically, financially and in terms of resident lay leadership. In addition, the community of political interest between Nonconformity and the working classes was increasingly under strain in the last quarter of the century. In the campaign for the Second Reform Act, political Nonconformity took for granted that it was the natural ally of working-class discontent, in a common attack upon the entrenched position of the Establishment, both political and religious. By the end of the century that community of interest was gone: on the one hand, the emergence of an independent Labour interest split the cohesion of the Nonconformist political outlook: how far now should the chapel speak for Labour, how free was it to liberate itself from the Liberal alliance, how far did a chapel, much less a denomination, have an agreed political policy? Conversely, the Nonconformist moralistic programme of political engagement was either peripheral or antipathetic to working men's interests: they had more immediate matters of concern than undenominational education, temperance, and Disestablishment. The Liberal-Nonconformist Alliance was now working to the disadvantage of both parties: 'liberalism in the 1890s' in J. F. Glaser's words 'appeared to many working-class voters as a Crochet Castle, from which dreary teetotalling Dissenters launched raids on pubs, music halls and politicians cited in divorce cases'.[10] For its part dissent without disabilities seemed to many working-class leaders to have become part of the Establishment and to be open to the same objections. Indeed it is to be wondered whether the aggressive Dissenters of the mid-century with their strategies for assaulting the fortress of Establishment would have owned as children

[10] J. F. Glaser, 'English Nonconformity and the Decline of Liberalism' in *American Historical Review* (1958), p. 359.

the prosperous, complacent and even smug Nonconformists of the end of the century caricatured by Arnold Bennett: perhaps they were only stepchildren, for somehow, conveniently, the old prophetic voice had been muted.

1

NONCONFORMITY AND THE INDIVIDUAL

The individual Dissenter trod out an earthly pilgrimage of mingled sorrows and spiritual delights, distinguished by singularity of purpose and tenacity of conviction. Their Dissenting childhoods are remembered rather differently by the Reverend Brewin Grant (**A**(i)), a Congregational minister of humble origins whose sympathetic portrait is all the more remarkable in that in later life his attitude to Nonconformity was sour and critical, and by the progeny of the Reverend John Clayton (**A**(ii)), one of the most aristocratic of metropolitan Dissenting ministers in the earliest years of the century.

Within adolescence or early manhood, a decisive turning-point was expected in the Nonconformist's experience: the Strict Baptist John Kershaw (**B**(i)), of social status even more lowly than Grant, describes his conversion movingly (and Calvinistically). The majority of Evangelical Dissenters in the early part of the century underwent such experiences, as Charles Kingsley, from a different tradition well understood (**B**(ii)), but as the century progressed, their intensity was heightened in the humbler classes especially by an experience of the 'second blessing' (common from the 1840s onwards), but diminished in the direction of greater refinement and intellectuality of response in the upper strata.

In contradistinction to that Calvinism which put strict confines upon the numbers of the elect, there was also a dissent, powerfully influenced by the Methodist Revival, which proclaimed a gospel available to every individual (**C**). To this Arminianism the older Calvinism in its 'modified' or 'moderate' version gradually approximated as the century wore on. Anti-nomianism in the nineteenth century represented little more than a label of polemical abuse: the long years of manhood and domestic duty saw no lightening of religious responsibility. 'Justification' had now to be realized in a 'sanctification' of daily life. Whilst Hugh Stowell Brown, a Liverpool Baptist, discusses with equal authoritativeness the secular and spiritual progress expected of a Dissenter in his maturity (**D**), J. Baldwin Brown, who deserves to be remembered as much for his sympathetic sociological commentaries on Dissenting life as for his advanced liberal theology, provides the guide-lines for the kind of household pattern which the Nonconformist paterfamilias was expected to uphold (**E**).

In contrast to Baldwin Brown's worldly wisdom James Montgomery's hymn upon prayer (**F**), much loved and sung within the century, articulates the principal 'means of grace' available to the individual Christian in his pilgrimage: without the daily prayer-watch he knew himself to be lost in a world in which so many hostile forces were ranged against him.

Finally, since happy deaths as much as agonizing conversions were matters of principal concern to Victorian Dissenters, that is, if their literature is at all a guide in these matters, two typical death-bed scenes are extracted from the pages of the *Primitive Methodist Magazine*. Once again, however, it should be recalled that Dissent runs through the whole gamut of English society below the peerage: the upper middle-class Congregationalist or Presbyterian, still less the Unitarian, while just as concerned with the process of dying, would not relish the experience being described quite so minutely or fulsomely as this (**G**)

A   Childhood

(i)   Taking the south side of Leicester as the starting point and travelling on by Aylestone and Blaby, continuing the journey some six miles in all, we arrive at the village of Countesthorpe, at least it *was* a village then, when I was born in it, on the 3rd of April, 1821.

My father and mother were attendants at the 'Meeting' and were 'members of the Church' worshipping in it. 'We lads' all of course attended and were in the Sunday School. . . .

My father was the priest of his household, a man of deep and earnest religious spirit, and as well acquainted with the Bible as any one I have ever met with. I have no doubt I can say for my four brothers who live in Leicester, that if ever in some unhappy mood we were disposed to say with the Psalmist 'all men are liars', the remembrance of this sterling example would silence our scepticism.

I believe my father's early religious awakening was produced in connection with the sermons of some Calvinistic clergyman. I remember him speaking highly of, I think, two names, Vaughan and Robinson, of this class, who were frequently instrumental in guiding him in his early youth to the Saviour, in whom he believed with a faith and cheerfulness which no sorrows or troubles ever beclouded; for though no man enjoyed life more, or more overflowed with constant thankfulness for 'temporal mercies', and a serene joy as to his future inheritance, on which he constantly drew, so that if he had been in prison or a workhouse, he would have felt that his palace was next door, and that he was only waiting his Father's time to enter—still he had his sorrows and bereavements and struggles as all men have. His greatest anxiety was to see his children 'walking in the truth'; and if he had had in one hand the gift of a splendid fortune and in the other the gift of God which is eternal life, to bestow only one or the other of them on us, we should have had the latter. I have two distinct early pictures of him, in this respect, one, as we walked alongside him in the fields on Sunday afternoon, asking us, I think out of a catechism called 'Milk For Babes' —'Can you tell me, child, who made you?' To which the answer was, as I remember, 'The Great God who made heaven and earth'; the other picture is that of his frequently standing at our bed's foot, earnestly speaking to us and praying for us. There was many a wet pillow of which he was ignorant, as the dusk of some summer evening deepened, and we could just discern his form, by the remaining light that streamed into our cottage chamber.

The changes of trade—from alteration in machinery in manufactur-ing wool into yarn—drove my father into the wilderness of this world to follow the tide of emigration from villages to the towns. For some time he went as a pioneer to Leicester, leaving us lads with our mother, whom we all loved and never vexed. . . . My father came home on the Saturday evening, and Sunday was a good day for us. The first thing for which we felt before quite awake was a 'plum bun' by our pillows. . . .

As to education we had but ordinary school advantages, though we were all given to reading. I was two years in St Margaret's school, Leicester, much of the time serving as 'Monitor'; and a few of us were favoured by Mr Hackett, the very efficient and gentlemanly 'master', with extra private teaching, in grammar and other subjects. . . .

I left that school to keep the books of a small stocking manufacturer, who took out work from hosiers and employed men in 'frames' of his own, for which he received weekly rent. . . .

In the place where I was there were several books which I read with avidity—some volumes of Chambers' *Journal*, a copy of Adam Smith's *Theory of Moral Sentiments*, a Shakespeare, Lavater's *Physiognomy*, with plates, and *Boxiana*! To these I added Watts' *Improvement of the Mind*, Cowper's *Poems*, then my especial favourites, and Young's *Night Thoughts*. . . .

During my discursive reading at the age of about 17, I became much interested in the Unitarian controversy. I sat up many nights till very late, writing down my arguments on the subject and upon the general doctrines of Christianity. My father frequently remonstrated with me for being so late. His favourite phrase on retiring was 'you will be like a dead thing in the morning'. At last he discovered my manuscript, and without my knowledge took it to the Reverend Dr Legge. The

Doctor professed to discover some sign of promise in the papers thus surreptitiously obtained, and sent for me and enquired into my religious views, and whether I had any desire to become a minister.

Brewin Grant, *The Dissenting World, An Autobiography* (1869), 9–15.

(ii) From the commencement of the day to its close, order and method reigned in the household. Reference has been made to the regularity with which the devotional exercises of the family were conducted. These, in the morning, scarcely ever exceeded fifteen minutes, as he [the Reverend John Clayton] deemed that amount of time sufficiently long, when little children and servants were to take part in the act of worship.

Breakfast despatched, there immediately followed what might be called the morning lecture. First, a chapter was read by the children, and briefly commented upon by the father, and illustrated by images and anecdotes level to their capacities. Afterwards selections were made from Watts' *Lyrics*, Cowper's *Poems*, the *Odyssey* of Homer, as versified by that author, Pope's *Iliad*, and the *Dramas* of Hannah More; and the reading of these was interspersed with remarks of a moral and religious character.

Pains were taken to induce habits of reflection, and every encouragement given to young people, to speak out what they thought, with unrestrained freedom and familiarity. This method of eliciting their own sentiments—often, doubtless, crude and immature, and even wild—presented to him the opportunity of correcting what was erroneous, and commending what was sound and true, although it might be imperfectly conceived and expressed.

Mr. Clayton accustomed his children to read to him aloud, and to recite passages of prose and poetry which they had committed to memory. On these occasions he would instruct them in the art of speaking; explaining and exemplifying the several rules of articulation, emphasis and the modulations of the voice. He advised that they should follow nature in these respects, as opposed to what is merely artificial. . . .

When Mr Clayton had finished with his children, he went forth either to his study or some engagement connected with his pastoral and public duties. These occupied the intervals of meals, and were agreeably diversified by recreation, physical and mental, alone or with his family, until the evening of the day brought with it the season for those hallowed exercises, social and secret, with which it appropriately closed.

The hour from eight to nine was, for many years, set apart for the private devotions of the family—visitors and servants being included in this arrangement. Each retired to his own room, for the perusal of the Scriptures and prayer; and thus a period was allotted to those duties, before weariness had incapacitated for their efficient discharge; and a sweet preparation was enjoyed for the family exercise which followed. Thrice blessed the household that is thus governed! 'Happy is that people that is in such a case; yea, happy is that people whose God is their Lord!'

While the ordinary occupations of the week went on, the Sabbath brought its own special privileges and duties. . . .

In the important matter of Family Discipline—so necessary to be kept up; so difficult to keep up wisely and well, with the preservation of the happy medium between undue laxity and unjust severity—Mr Clayton sought counsel at the lips of the 'God of all the families of Israel', who has said, 'If any of you lack wisdom, let him ask of God, that giveth to all men liberally and upbraideth not.'

It was a favourite phrase with him that the Bible ought to be the chief magistrate in every house, and the authority whose judgment should be final, in all cases that might arise. He particularly recommended the book of Proverbs; and encouraged those around him to commit to memory portions of that repository of piety, wisdom and sound morality; and thus to retain its sage counsels for practical purposes in future life. He often referred to passages of that book in order to explain those acts of discipline which he felt it his duty to administer. The rod, suitably applied in case of grievous faults, especially when persisted in, after kindly admonition, he regarded to be nothing less than an ordinance of God, for the right training of children. The horsewhip, whose place was the architrave of the door of his study, was seldom used for correction, but often pointed to, as 'the silver-headed monitor'. . . .

Very early did she [Mrs John Clayton] wish her children to recognize the sacredness of the Lord's Day, and to love it. She obliged us to put away all our toys at six on Saturday afternoon. She found pleasing and entertaining books, suited to our age; and used to narrate to us the historical parts of Scripture in her own language, and we were to guess the names of the persons. Every Sabbath evening she was accustomed to gather us around her, taking the youngest on her lap, and ask us very close questions, about our thoughts and feelings; and pray with us, in most simple and tender language. Perhaps the very first convictions of sin in the heart, and the desire to have it pardoned and subdued, may be dated from these seasons of maternal watchfulness and love. . . .

She loved to be the companion of her sons and daughters, and to get their confidence as well as affection. When it became twilight, before the candles were brought, she delighted to amuse and instruct us, and to call our mental faculties into exercise. She went through the various tribes of bird, beast, fish, plants and trees, asking each child in turn what was its favourite, and why he or she liked that best, and when we had selected ours (some for form, or beauty of plumage, or fine singing etc.), she would tell us which was her choice, and give substantial reasons for valuing it; bringing out useful qualities, or gentle manners, and thus leading us to estimate most highly what benefitted or delighted society, rather than what merely attracted the eye by the showy and extrinsic.

She was anxious, at the very earliest period, to subdue the will, but on no account to break the spirit. She said the duties, cares and trials of future life would call for all the cheerfulness and buoyancy that any young one possessed; and therefore it was wise to keep the spirit as firm and unbroken as possible, but to induce, as soon as could be, the self-denial, self-relinquishment, meekness and gentleness which the religion of Jesus taught. Once, when two of the children had quarrelled violently, one of them said, 'Mama, I cannot bear to be so treated.'

'My dear,' she replied, 'you must learn to bear whatever God pleases to appoint. Even the ill-temper and harshness of others you must quietly endure, that you may gain patience and forbearance. Now I desire you to go up into your room, and open the Testament, and pray over those words, 'Learn of me: for I am meek and lowly in heart: and ye shall find rest to your souls." And I charge you not to come downstairs to me, till you have wept and pleaded over that text; and till you have a hope that the gentle spirit of Jesus is in a measure given to you.'

The child did so, and that was an occurrence that remained in the memory, as a waymark in life's history: for never was such petulance again felt; and never again was there a quarrel between the two, who were then so angry with each other.

T. W. Aveling, Memorials of the Clayton Family (1867), 100–105, 387–9, on the Reverend John Clayton senior, and Mrs John Clayton junior, his daughter-in-law

B Conversion

(i) *An inside view*

I hope never to forget the night the Lord brought my soul out of
bondage into the glorious liberty of the gospel. It was on a Lord's Day
evening. I went in the morning to the house of God in a very distressed
state of mind, and remained so all day. The preaching only tended to
increase my misery, the enemy telling me that, like Simon Magus, I had
neither part nor lot in the matter. Having attended three services I was
returning home (it was a fine summer evening) in my feelings worse
than when I set out in the morning. So sinful, wretched and miserable
did I feel myself that I was ready to give up all for lost, the accuser of
the brethren harassing me with his temptations, saying that it was of
no use going any more either to chapel or prayer meetings. It was folly,
he suggested, and presumption to read and pray, for the more I attended
to these things the more wretched I grew.

My soul gave way under these temptations, and I said within myself,
'I will give all religion up, for it is nothing but a stench in my nostrils.
What must it then be to the Lord of Hosts?' So engaged was my mind
that I stood still in the road, when this question came to me 'What am I
to do? Go back into the world I cannot. I have tried again and again to
do that, and found it more and more distasteful.' I then concluded
that I would have nothing to do either with the world or with the
people of God, but be a kind of go-between, and try to make myself as
easy as possible in my present condition; but alas! there is no comfort
for a guilty sinner in such a state of mind.

While I was thinking about these things, the following words came
with such power upon my mind, that it was as though I had heard them
spoken with an audible voice: 'Oh wretched man that I am, who shall
deliver me from this body of sin and death?' I was so struck with their
impact that I stood amazed, saying to myself, 'These are the words of
St. Paul in the seventh chapter to the Romans. He was a good and
gracious man, a minister of Jesus Christ, and the great apostle to the
Gentiles. If he had thus to complain of sin and wretchedness, who can
tell but I may be a child of God after all my fears and temptations?' The
latter part of that chapter flowed into my mind like a river. I could try,
say, 'For that which I do I allow not; for what I would, that do I not;
for what I hate, that I do. I find then a law, that when I would do good,
evil is present with me.'

My soul was a greatly encouraged. I found I was a brother and companion with Paul in this path of internal tribulation and Christian experience. I hastened home to get my Bible, in order to examine the chapter through. I read it with such light, power and comfort as I had never felt before; so pleased and blest in my soul that I began to read the next chapter, commencing thus; 'There is, therefore now no condemnation to them which are in Christ Jesus, who walk not after the flesh but after the Spirit.'

As I read these precious words, their blessed contents were brought into my soul with power and glory. I saw and felt that I was in Christ Jesus, saved with an everlasting salvation. The burden of sin was removed and my conscience cleansed by an application of the precious blood of Jesus Christ. I felt the sealing testimony of the Holy Spirit of God that I stood complete and accepted in the Beloved. I read the chapter through with a joy I cannot describe. I now knew my election of God, and that no charge could ever be brought against me, because Christ had died for my sins, and been raised again from the dead for my justification; that He ever lived to make intercession for me, and would receive me into his kingdom of glory. The love of Christ was shed abroad in my heart; I saw and felt that nothing could separate me from the love of God, which is in Christ Jesus our Lord. How precious and glorious were the truths contained in that chapter to my soul on that memorable evening.

Thanking the Lord for the great deliverance he had wrought for me and in me, I retired for the night with the joy of salvation in my soul, but I was so ravished with the beauty and glory of Christ as my Saviour and Redeemer, that sleep left me. I had previously endured many restless nights with a guilty conscience, a broken law, an evil heart, a tempting devil, crowds of doubts and fears and carnal reasonings; but all had now departed. The year of jubilee was come, the prisoner was brought out of the dungeon into the banqueting house, and the banner over him was love. I well remember the question passing across my mind:'Where are all my sins, that have so long been a burden and plague to my soul?' I saw by faith that a precious Christ had put them all away by the sacrifice of Himself, and made an end of sin. They had appeared as scarlet and crimson, but were all washed away in the blood of atonement. As I stood in Christ, I was as white as snow or as wool.

John Kershaw, *The Autobiography of an Eminent Lancashire Preacher* (1968 reprint), 62–3

(ii) *An outside view*

I used, as I said, to call it the curse of circumstance that I was a sickly,
decrepit Cockney. My mother used to tell me that it was the cross
which God had given me to bear. I know now that she was right there.
She used to say that my disease was God's will. I do not think, though,
that she spoke right there also. I think that it was the will of the world
and of the devil, of man's avarice, and laziness, and ignorance. And
so would my readers, perhaps had they seen the shop in the city where
I was born and nursed, with its little garrets reeking with human
breath, its kitchens and areas with noisome sewers. A sanitary reformer
would not be long in guessing the cause of my unhealthiness. He would
not rebuke me—nor would she, sweet soul! now that she is at rest in
bliss—for my wild longings to escape, for my envying the very flies
and sparrows their wings that I might flee miles away into the country,
and breathe the air of heaven once, and die. I have had my wish, I
have made two journeys far away into the country, and they have
been enough for me.

My mother was a widow, my father, whom I cannot recollect, was
a small retail tradesman in the city. He was unfortunate; and when he
died, my mother came down, and lived penuriously enough, I knew
not how till I grew older, down in that same suburban street. She had
been brought up an Independent. After my father's death she became a
Baptist, from conscientious scruples. She considered the Baptists, as I
do, as the only sect who thoroughly embody the Calvinistic doctrines.
She held it as I do, an absurd and impious thing for those who believe
mankind to be children of the devil till they have been consciously
'converted', to baptise unconscious infants and give them the sign of
God's mercy on the mere chance of that mercy being intended for them.
When God had proved, by converting them, that they were not reprobate and doomed to hell by His absolute and eternal will, then, and
not till then, dare man baptise them into His name. She dared not palm
a presumptuous fiction on herself, and call it 'charity'. So, though we
had both been christened during my father's lifetime, she purposed to
have us rebaptised, if ever that happened—which, in her sense of the
word, never happened, I am afraid, to me.

She gloried in her dissent, for she was sprung from old Puritan blood,
which had flowed again and again beneath the knife of Star-Chamber
butchers, and on the battlefields of Naseby and Sedgemoor. And on
winter evenings she used to sit with her Bible on her knee, while I and
my little sister Susan, stood beside her and listened to the stories of

Gideon and Barak, and Samson and Jephthah, till her eye kindled up, and her thoughts passed forth from that old Hebrew time home into those English times which she fancied, and not untruly, like them. And we used to shudder, and yet listen with a strange fascination, as she told us how her ancestor called his seven sons off their small Cambridge farm, and horsed and armed them himself to follow behind Cromwell, and smite kings and prelates with 'the sword of the Lord and of Gideon'. Whether she were right or wrong, what is it to me? What is it now to her, thank God? But those stories, and the strict, stern Puritan education, learnt from the Independents and not the Baptists, which accompanied them, had their effect on me, for good and ill.

My mother moved by rule and method; by God's law, as she considered, and that only. She seldom smiled. Her word was absolute. She never commanded twice without punishing. And yet there were abysses of unspoken tenderness in her, as well as clear, sound, womanly sense and insight. But she thought herself as much bound to keep down all tenderness as if she had been some ascetic of the Middle Ages—so do extremes meet! It was 'carnal' she considered. She had as yet no right to have any 'spiritual affection' for us. We were still 'children of wrath and of the devil'—not yet 'convinced of sin', 'converted, born again'. She had no more spiritual bond with us, she thought, than she had with a heathen or a Papist. She dared not even pray for our conversion, earnestly as she prayed on every other subject. For though the majority of her sect would have done so, her clear logical sense would yield to no such tender inconsistency. Had it not been decided from all eternity? We were elect, or we were reprobate. Could her prayers alter that? If He had chosen us, He would call us in His own good time: and, if not—Only, again and again, as I afterwards discovered from a journal of hers, she used to beseech God with agonized tears to set her mind at rest by revealing to her His will towards us. For that comfort she could at least rationally pray. But she received no answer. Poor, beloved mother! If thou couldst not read the answer, written in every flower and every sunbeam, written in the very fact of our existence here at all, what answer would have sufficed thee?

And yet, with all this, she kept the strictest watch over our morality. Fear, of course, was the only motive she employed; for how could our still carnal understandings be affected with love to God? And love to herself was too paltry and temporary to be urged by one who knew that her life was uncertain, and who was always trying to go down to the deepest eternal ground and reason of everything, and take her stand upon that. So our god, or gods rather, till we were twelve years old,

were hell, the rod, the ten commandments, and public opinion. Yet
under them, not they, but something deeper far, both in her and us,
preserved us pure.

C. Kingsley, *Alton Locke* (1850), 2–4

C A gospel for all

WELCOME, welcome! sinner, hear!
Hang not back through shame or fear:
Doubt not, nor distrust the call;
Mercy is proclaimed to all.

Welcome to the offered peace;
Welcome, prisoner, to release:
Burst thy bonds; be saved; be free!
Rise and come—He calleth thee.

Welcome, weeping penitent!
Grace has made thy heart relent:
Welcome, long estranged child!
God in Christ is reconciled.

Welcome to the cleansing fount
Springing from the sacred mount;
Welcome to the feast divine,
Bread of life, and living wine.

All ye weary and distrest!
Welcome to relief and rest;
All is ready; hear the call;
There is ample room for all.

None can come that shall not find
Mercy called whom Grace inclined!
Nor shall any willing heart
Hear the bitter word—Depart!

O! the virtue of that price.
That redeeming sacrifice!
Come, ye bought, but not with gold,
Welcome to the sacred fold.

JOSIAH CONDER. 1836
Psalms and Hymns (1899), no. 344

D   Progress: secular and spiritual

Text: 'And the Lord said unto Moses, Wherefore criest thou unto Me? Speak unto the children of Israel that they go forward' (Exodus xiv, 15).

... Our text furnishes us with an admirable motto for the present season, the beginning of a new year. Forward is the word which I should now like to ring in every ear and every heart—forward in all that is true, and just, and good.

There is a secular sense in which this motto may be understood and very usefully employed, as expressive of the desire and determination to make progress in the world, to achieve success in business, to grapple with and overcome every obstacle that stands in the way of such advancement. And to this application of our motto, I am so far from entertaining any objection, that I wish it were far more than it is the rule approved, adopted and carried out by every man.

If it were so there would be much less poverty and wretchedness in the world, and I firmly believe much less sin, for the course of life that leads to secular success is a course of life that requires the cultivation of many excellent qualities, and the exercise of much self-denial and self-control; and as it is a course of life that leaves no room for idleness, this alone guarantees the avoidance of much wickedness.

It may be said that the man who wishes to get on in the world, and bends his energies in this direction, exposes himself to many temptations, and this is true; but it is equally true that temptations, to the full as many, as strong and as injurious, beset the man who leads a trifling, careless and comparatively idle life. And although it may be objected that a life of intense application to secular business and great activity in the pursuit of success is likely to make a man wordly-minded, I don't hesitate to say, as a result of my observation and knowledge of man, that the indolent and the unsuccessful down to the very pauper in the workhouse, are quite as wordly-minded as those who are most diligent and prosperous. I firmly believe that he who is diligent in business is more likely than he who is slothful in business to be fervent in spirit, serving the Lord. God's service needs the minds that are sharpened and brightened by the activities of business life; God's service requires the help that prosperity is able to afford. And therefore I have no fear, no hesitation in expressing the desire that every one of you may in this secular sense go forward, and have a year of progress and prosperity in the things of this present world.

Poor health, the expense of bringing up a large family, the advance of age with its infirmities, constitute a continual struggle; and if some such sorely pressed men be here, I desire to express the very sincere sympathy which I feel for them.

But, my brothers, in this life's battle, this motto, though it may seem to mock you when taken in a secular sense, has a far greater meaning in which it does not mockingly speak to you. In regard to making progress in moral and spiritual things, in regard to the aquisition of the best riches, of what, according to Jesus Christ are the only true, the only real riches, you stand on the same footing with those who have the finest opportunities of advancement in the world. And I ask you to assert your self-respect, and if the world respect none but the worldly rich, don't you echo back such a contemptible and abominable sentiment by repining, on the ground that comparatively mean circumstances, from which you cannot escape, keep you down and keep you back. Neither a man's life nor a man's worth consisteth in the abundance of the things that he possesseth. And if you cannot go forward in the direction of money-making, be all the more resolved to go forward in the direction of acquiring the riches of righteousness and grace and glory. If on the lower level your path is blocked up, try the higher level, the more intellectual, the more spiritual level, that is never blocked to any earnest man—progress, useful progress, progress to any extent, is always possible there.

Hugh Stowell Brown, *Manliness and Other Sermons* (1889), 357–62

E Domesticity

Now from the first, far back as we can trace the *origiones* of our race, the household was the true unit of German society, the man lord in his home, which was his castle against the world, the woman his coequal and helpmeet in counsel, rule and even in war, the children his charge both of burden and joy, with slight right or power on the part of the community to intervene and limit his discretion in the government of his patriarchal realm. . . . We number our people by their families as God numbered his people of old. The number of pure, living and happy families in the bosom of merry England has always been, and still is, the measure of the strength and stability of our state. The home-life of England has, we believe, been her main safeguard against the excesses of revolution, while the undomestic and out-door life of neighbouring continental peoples has had no little to do with the swift and fierce revolutionary fury which has, again and again, seized them, and set well-nigh the whole world in a blaze. An Englishman's home is his castle, not against the tyrant only, but against the genius, or shall we say, the demon, of Revolution, and long may holy and happy home-life insure the stability of our institutions on the one hand, and minister to the orderly and peaceful development of our national life on the other.

And this 'domestic character' is passing through its searching trial, equally with the 'spirit of liberty' and the 'religious mind', with which it is happily blended still. Were we prepared to accept as final the judgments of the able but sardonic weekly review of which the *aura* of the clubs seems to be the inspiration, we should write Ichabod over the doors of our homes, and believe that their glory was faded for ever. Nothing can be sadder than the picture of mothers and daughters, and of the way in which brothers, lovers and husbands regard them, which is constantly paraded before the most intelligent and cultivated section of the community as the likeness of English domestic life. And we believe, sorrowfully enough, that there is that before the eyes of the writers among the upper ten thousand which lends the form of truth to the image which they portray. Anything more low, heartless and undomestic than the habit of life of a great section of English society, which claims the honour of the 'prerogative tribe', it would be difficult to conceive; though even here, an observer with a domestic eye might find many bright lights to mitigate the gloom of the hues which he employs. But happily for us, we have no prerogative tribe in England. It may seem like a paradox, but we believe that nowhere in the world does an aristocracy enjoy such true honour and wield such wide-spreading influence as in England; and yet nowhere in the world does an aristocracy less monopolize the ruling influences and forces of the state. The great middle class, as it is called in England, is a thing by itself. Chiefly, perhaps, in that it is not a class, but is fully penetrated without being possessed by the influence of the classes above and beneath. It is this middle class which is the true core of the community; this makes and saves the state. And in this vast core of English society the domestic character still reigns, but slightly, if at all, impaired. Pater-familias and materfamilias are still very substantial and influential entities in the thick middle stratum of the British nation, and hearty, healthy-minded boys and girls (the latter neither nymphs nor butter-cups) abound. We believe that the the intensely artificial life which characterizes what is called society, and which seems to grow more artificial daily, has hardly touched the great mass of our households with its withering breath. . . . As far as our observation and information extend, the homes of England are still as substantially sound and healthy as in the great Puritan days, though we cannot hide from ourselves that influences are at work very powerfully in our days, which threaten to invade and rifle the most sacred shrine of our temple—that which bears the twice-consecrated name of home.

There is a school of politicians which professes greatly to dread the Americanizing of our institutions. Perhaps we have more need to be on our guard against the Americanizing of our domestic life. Boys and girls are scarce in America. Precocious maturity and precocious independence make sad havoc in our homes. We have no room to consider the special influences which are acting on the home life of our first cousins in the New World, producing results which thoughtful American writers regard with grave apprehension. We have to guard, in a measure, against the same dangers. In our manufacturing districts kindred conditions are developing the same tendencies. We have heard the remark from thoughtful observers of the life of our working classes in the cotton districts, that the cotton famine brought with it one rich compensation for all the woe it wrought, in that it taught men and women—yes, and children too—to understand, as they had never before had the chance of understanding, the meaning of the word home. Still, in spite of the pressure of circumstances, the domestic character which is ingrained in our people bears up bravely under the strain. Some of the purest, healthiest and happiest homes in England are to be found in those very districts, nor could they, in fairness, be selected as the districts in which, looking at the character of the whole community, the domestic feeling has been most impaired or destroyed.

But we cannot but fear that the intellectual movement of our times is acting, in many respects, detrimentally to our domestic life. The immense preponderance of the light element in our staple literary production, and the ease with which the cream of knowledge can be skimmed by young people, from popular treatises and magazines, foster that mental and moral precocity which is sadly detrimental to the domestic character wherever it is found largely developed. It is a bad thing, from this domestic point of view—and it is one of the highest points of view—to push young people on, physically, mentally, or morally, too fast. Keep boys boys, and girls girls, as long as possible. They will make the nobler and stronger men and women through blooming somewhat late.

J. Baldwin Brown, 'The Domestic Character of Englishmen' in *The Evangelical Magazine*, Volume 10 (New Series, 1868), 584–6

F 'The Christian's Vital Breath'

PRAYER is the soul's sincere desire,
   Uttered or unexprest!
The motion of a hidden fire,
   That trembles in the breast.

Prayer is the burden of a sigh,
   The falling of a tear,
The upward glancing of an eye,
   When none but God is near.

Prayer is the simplest form of speech
   That infant lips can try;
Prayer, the sublimest strains that reach
   The Majesty on high.

Prayer is the Christian's vital breath,
   The Christian's native air:
His watchword at the gates of death,—
   He enters heaven with prayer.

Prayer is the contrite sinner's voice,
   Returning from his ways:
While angels in their songs rejoice,
   And cry, "Behold, he prays!"

The saints, in prayer, appear as one,
   In word, and deed, and mind;
While, with the Father and the Son,
   Sweet fellowship they find.

Nor prayer is made on earth alone;
   The Holy Spirit pleads;
And Jesus, on the eternal throne,
   For mourners intercedes.

O Thou, by whom we come to God,
   The Life, the Truth, the Way!
The path of prayer Thyself hast trod:
   Lord, teach us how to pray!

JAMES MONTGOMERY, 1819.
Psalms and Hymns (1899), no. 860

G Death

(i) In his 55th year this is the way in which Mr Collins finished his journey—'Blessed be God that ever I was born! Blessed be God who hath washed me in his precious blood! Thanks be to God who giveth us the victory through Christ Jesus our Lord. O God, I have delighted in Thy precepts! That law of Thine, "Thou shalt love the Lord thy God with all thy heart", Thou hast made dear to me. According to Thy Covenant Thou hast put it into my mind. O! Thy power to save to the uttermost. I have not been a timid witness.

Satan! I have done with him. I have resisted him and he flees from me. Jesus, my All in All Thou art. I am in Thy hands, loving Saviour. In these final struggles perfect me in patience. Let me lack nothing. *As* Thou wilt, *what* Thou wilt, *when* Thou wilt. I leave it all to Thee.

By how many mercies am I surrounded! From how many pains delivered! O Lord, since I dedicated myself to Thee and to Thy Ministry, Thou knowest that I have not wickedly departed from Thee. Pardon my shortcomings. I wash me in the Blood of Jesus. O my Shepherd, my smitten Shepherd! by Thy stripes am I healed. I know it; let the attestations of my short life terminate there.' Believing in the Lord Jesus, he confidently, peacefully, triumphantly, and therefore gloriously, completed his earthly pilgrimage.

(ii) One of our rising young authoresses has been called to her rest. 'Ruth Elliot' was the daughter of the Reverend Mr Peck, Wesleyan minister of Chelmsford. Although only 28 years old, she had gained her laurels as a Christian novelist. . . . She seemed to feel a great dread of the estate of death the very day before she departed; but in her last hour this quiet, calm, meditative spirit was alive with joy. She had taken no stimulant, no narcotic, nothing to create from the physical side such an experience. These were her words at one o'clock at night—

'I am going, going home. Yes, I know I am, and Jesus is near—close by in this room. You can't see Him, but I can clearly, and He is touching me. He is holding me up, and so strongly, I fear nothing. I have no terror! Don't be afraid for me! O, I can see it all now! I can see inside, and it is lovely, lovely! O, I never saw anything so lovely. It is so easy to die, so very easy. There is nothing in the world easier than to die. I wish I'd gone long ago for such happiness as this.' 'The everlasting arms are around you,' said one. 'Yes, and under me too,' she said. 'Jesus is so very close; all of you believe me. O, it is most lovely! I want to go; it won't be very long, will it? No pain, no pain, not any more pain. O Jesus, Keep me close till I get right in! There's nothing like this beautiful heaven! I am nearly there! I see Jesus!' And with a last look of ineffable peace, she closed her eyes. . . .

Her last reading had been Miss Martineau's biography, and had she lived, she intended to give a record of a kind of psychological experience of an opposite extreme, from her own heart-book. She rests now in Abney Park cemetery, in her quiet tomb; but her pure soul is with God.

Obituary notices, *Primitive Methodist Magazine* (1878), 734-5

2

NONCONFORMITY AND
THE CHURCH

The wide range of different social types and classes embraced by Victorian Dissent can be detected in the variety of styles of worship encountered. Mrs Gaskell's fictional portrait in her novel *Ruth* (**A**(i)) is based on the Unitarian chapel at Knutsford, the quiet and semi-rural Cheshire town of her childhood. In contrast Mrs Oliphant describes a prosperous city church in her little-known novel *Phoebe Junior* (**A**(ii)). A down-town Free Methodist chapel in Manchester (**A**(iii)) is the subject of the third extract, and a Primitive Methodist cause in a Durham mining village of the fourth (**A**(iv)).

Despite the loosening of classical Dissenting polity and the theological laxity of the nineteenth century, church discipline remained rigorous, probably because Puritan morality long outlasted Puritan theology and church organization. The Reverend J. Angus, a Baptist, rebuts objections to its continued functioning in a work published in 1862 (**B**(i)), whilst the minute book of Pembroke Baptist Church, Liverpool (**B**(ii)), shows it being applied moderately and charitably with respect to some of the more frequent lapses—absenteeism, intemperance, 'gross sin', bankruptcy and mixed marriages—which occasioned its exercise in Victorian times.

The Dissenting ministry of the same period has been variously judged: Dickens' odious types contrast strongly with the attractive heroes of Mrs Oliphant's *Salem Chapel*, George Eliot's *Felix Holt* or Mrs Gaskell's short story *Cousin Phyllis*. Dr Bennett, writing in 1839, suggests a vigorous intellectual elite of assured social standing, pursuing active and interesting careers (**C**(i)). J. A. James and J. P. Mursell (**C**(ii)) suggest that a different calling awaited the minister of meagre talents, compelled to serve humble, ill-bred and money-grubbing congregations; other ministers however found positive advantage in the same system (**C**(iii)), whilst Joseph Parker censures those who use their deacons as scapegoats for their own inadequacies (**C**(iv)). At the turn of the century W. F. Adeney, the Congregationalist theologian, depicted the minister overworked to breaking point, baffled and bewildered as the pace of congregational enlightenment outstripped his intellectual development (**C**(v)). In practice, it seems probable that more often the reverse was true—many of the crises in late Victorian chapels, as Dr Clyde Binfield has shown, occurred because the minister was out-thinking his more conservative flock.[1]

The union of hitherto autonomous churches into more compact fellowships, signalized by the creation and growth of the Congregational and Baptist Unions[2] and the development of subordinate local denominational organizations, was partly a response to the need to cater more methodically for increasing and mobile populations, partly an inevitable process in the rapid transition from sect to denominational status, and partly a response to Methodist connexional emphases and the unending Anglican critique of the follies and deficiencies of independency. An advocate of connexionalism like the Reverend Dr J. Thomas (**D**), widely suspected of attempting to import Presbyterianism into Congregationalism, expressed his point of view as loudly and dogmatically as any modern enthusiast for ecumenicalism: the latter movement is very much the twentieth-century version of the former.

Finally evidence is adduced for the judgment that the nineteenth century was so great an age of preaching and preachers, platform and pulpit oratory, with the congregation hearers rather than worshippers, passive recipients rather than partners in worship, that the great sacramental occasions (and sacramental teaching itself) fell into obscurity, if not into abeyance. Dr Pye Smith, the Congregationalist scholar, gives an analysis of the Lord's Supper, significantly enough in the very last pages of his *First Lines of Christian Theology or Lecture Notes for his Students*, which could hardly make less of the Sacrament (**E(i)**). Dr R. W. Dale (**E(ii)**), often acclaimed as the herald of a revival of High Sacramentalism among Congregationalists, seems more ingenious than convincing: a more substantial theology of the Lord's Supper had to await P. T. Forsyth. The Baptists, because of their distinctive rite, had to give it a more prominent place in their apologetics: the Reverend C. Williams of Accrington in his manual of Baptist principles is firmly scriptural (**E(iii)**)—even so a modern Baptist would miss any reference to the corporate significance of Baptism, or to the work of the Holy Spirit therein. Even among this most conservative of denominations, however, liberal thought made serious inroads: the Reverend Charles Aked (**E(iv)**) towards the end of the century, in a passage which also provides a good example of late Victorian evolutionary and immanentist preaching, somehow sees Believer's Baptism merely as a useful qualification for the social reformer.

Because its ecclesiology was so weak Old Dissent regarded with extreme disfavour religious bodies whose organization was rigid and unbending and which posed a threat to the liberties of free born Englishmen. Wesleyanism, not without justice, was regarded as among the worst of these (**F & G**): not till the latter half of the century when Wesleyanism had been mellowed by

[1] 'The Thread of Disruption: Some Nineteenth Century Churches in Eastern England', *Transactions of the Congregational Historical Society*, May 1967 and 'Chapels in Crisis', *ibid*, October 1968.

[2] The Baptist Union was founded in 1812 and reorganized with a revised constitution in 1832. The Congregational Union was founded in May 1832.

successive waves of sectarian blood-letting, did its chastened mood allow of a rapprochement with the rest of Dissent. An alternative explanation is that Wesleyanism never really mended its ways at all, but that Dissenting leaders merely gave in, and allowed it to impose its own centralized organization on the other denominations (see **D**).

Finally, Nonconformity is related to other forms of churchmanship—competition with fashionable Anglicanism through the adoption of liturgies and orders of worship, architectural conceits and visual symbolism, are illustrated from the pens of Nonconformists themselves and from that of Mr Gladstone in one of his rare comments on religious Dissent (**H**(i)–(iv)).

A   The Chapel

(i) *Rural Cheshire*

The Chapel was up a narrow street or rather, cul-de-sac, close by. It stood in the outskirts of the town, almost in the fields. It was built about the time of Philip and Matthew Henry, when the Dissenters were afraid of attracting attention or observation, and hid their places of worship in obscure and out-of-the-way parts of the towns in which they were built. Accordingly, it often happened, as in the present case, that the buildings immediately surrounding, as well as the chapels themselves, looked as if they carried you back to a period a hundred and fifty years ago. The chapel had a picturesque and old-world look, for luckily the congregation had been too poor to rebuild it, or new-face it, in George the Third's time. The staircases which led to the galleries were outside, at each end of the building, and the irregular roof and worn stone steps looked grey and stained by time and weather. The grassy hillocks, each with a little upright headstone, were shaded by a grand old wych-elm. A lilac-bush or two, a white rose-tree, and a few laburnums, all old and gnarled enough, were planted round the chapel yard, and the casement windows of the chapel were made of heavy-leaded, diamond-shaped panes, almost covered with ivy, producing a green gloom, not without its solemnity, within. This ivy was the home of an infinite number of little birds, which twittered and warbled, till it might have been thought that they were emulous of the power of praise possessed by the human creatures within, with such earnest, long-drawn strains did this crowd of winged songsters rejoice and be glad in their beautiful gift of life. The interior of the building was plain and simple, as plain and simple could be. When it was fitted up, oak-timber was much cheaper than it is now, so the wood-work was all of that description, but roughly-hewed, for the builders had not much wealth to spare. The walls were white-washed and were recipients of the shadows of the beauty without; on their 'white panes', the tracery of the ivy might be seen, now still, now stirred by the sudden flight of a little bird. The congregation consisted of here and there a farmer and his labourers, who came down from the uplands beyond the town to worship where their fathers worship-ped, and who loved the place because they knew how much those fathers had suffered for it, although they never troubled themselves with the reason why they left the parish church; and of a few shop-keepers, far more thoughtful and reasoning, who were Dissenters from conviction, unmixed with old, ancestral association; and of one or two families of still higher worldly station. With many poor, who were drawn there by love for Mr Benson's character, and by a feeling that the faith which made him what he was could not be far wrong, for the base of the pyramid, and with Mr Bradshaw for its apex, the congrega-tion stood complete.

The country people came in, sleeking down their hair, and treading with earnest attempts at noiseless lightness of step over the floor of the aisle; and, by and by, when all were assembled, Mr Benson followed, unmarshalled and unattended. When he had closed the pulpit door and knelt in prayer for an instant or two, he gave out a psalm from the dear old Scottish paraphrase, with its primitive inversion of the simple perfect Biblical words; and a kind of precentor stood up, and, having sounded the note on a pitch-pipe, sang a couple of lines by way of introducing the tune; then all the congregation stood up, and sang aloud, Mr Bradshaw's great bass voice being half a note in advance of the others, in accordance with his place of precedence as principal member of the congregation.

Mrs Gaskell, *Ruth* (1853) (Everyman, 1967 ed.), 151–2

(ii) *Suburban London*

Mr Beecham rose, like an actor, from a long and successful career in the Provinces, to what might be called the Surrey side of congrega-tional eminence in London; and from thence attained his final apothe-osis in a handsome chapel near Regent's Park, built of the whitest stone, and cushioned with the reddest damask, where a very large congregation sat in great comfort and listened to his sermons with a satisfaction no doubt increased by the fact that the cushions were soft as their own easy-chairs, and that carpets and hot-water pipes kept everything snug under foot.

It was the most comfortable chapel in the whole connection. The seats were arranged like those of an amphitheatre, each line on a slightly higher level than the one in front of it, so that everybody saw everything that was going on. No dimness or mystery was wanted there; everything was bright daylight, bright paint, red cushions, comfort and respectability. It might not be a place very well adapted for saying your prayers in, but then you could say your prayers at home— and it was a place admirably adapted for hearing sermons in, which you could not do at home; and all the arrangements were such that you could hear in the greatest comfort, not to say luxury. I wonder, for my own part, that the poor folk about did not seize upon Crescent Chapel on the cold Sunday mornings, and make themselves happy in those warm and ruddy pews. It would be a little amusing to speculate what all the well-dressed pew-holders would have done had this unexpected answer to the appeal which Mr Beecham believed himself to make every Sunday to the world in general, been literally given. It would have been extremely embarrassing to the Managing Committee and all the office-bearers, and would have, I fear, deeply exasperated and offended the occupants of those family pews; but fortunately, this difficulty never did occur. . . . The real congregation embraced none of the unwashed multitude. Its value in mere velvet, silk, lace, trinkets and furs was something amazing, and the amount these comfortable people represented in the way of income would have amounted to a most princely revenue. The little Salems and Bethesdas, with their humble flocks, could not be supposed to belong to the same species. . . . The pew-holders in Crescent Chapel were universally well-off; they subscribed liberally to missionary societies, far more liberally than the people at St Paul's close by did to the S.P.G. They had everything of the best in their chapel, as they did in their houses. They no more economised on their minister than they did on their pew-cushions, and they spent an amount of money on their choir which made the singing people at St Paul's gnash their teeth. . . . At the same time, they were what you might safely call well-informed people—people who read the newspapers, and sometimes the magazines, and knew what was going on. The men were almost all liberal in politics, and believed in Mr Gladstone with enthusiasm; the women often 'took an interest' in public movements, especially of a charitable character. There was less mental stagnation among them probably than among many of their neighbours. . . . Mr Beecham had many friends in the Law, and some even in the Broad Church. He appeared on platforms to promote various public movements along with clergymen of the Church. He spoke of 'our brethren within the pale of the Establishment', always with respect, sometimes even with enthusiasm. 'Depend upon it, my dear sir,' he would even say sometimes to a liberal brother, 'the Establishment is not such an unmitigated evil as some people consider it. What should we do in country parishes where the people are not awakened? They do the dirty work for us, my dear brother, the dirty work.' These sentiments were shared, but perhaps not warmly, by Mr Beecham's congregation, some of whom were hot Voluntaries, and gave their ministers a little trouble. But the most part took their Non-conformity very quietly, and were satisfied to know that their chapel was the first in the connection, and their minister justly esteemed as one of the most eloquent. The Liberation Society held one meeting at the Crescent Chapel, but it was not considered a great success. At the best, they were no more than lukewarm Crescent-chapelites, not political dissenters. Both minister and people were Liberal, that was the creed they professed. Some of the congregations citywards and the smaller chapels about Hampstead and Islington, used the word Latitudinarian instead; but that, as the Crescent Chapel people said, was a word always applied by the bigoted and ignorant to those who held in high regard the doctrines of Christian charity. They were indeed somewhat proud of their tolerance, their impartiality, their freedom from old prejudices 'That sort of thing will not do nowadays,' said Mr Copper-head, who was a great railway contractor, and one of the deacons and had a son at Oxford. If there had been any bigotry in the Crescent, Mr Copperhead would have had little difficulty in transferring himself over the way to St Paul's church, and it is astonishing what an effect that fact had on the mind of Mr Beecham's flock.

M. O. W. Oliphant, *Phoebe Junior* (1877 edn.), 3–8

(iii) *Down-town Manchester*

LEVER STREET U.M.F.C., MANCHESTER

The Lever Street Chapel stands a few yards from the corner of Ancoats Lane. We dismiss its external architecture with the remark that it belongs to the early order of Methodism, being simply an ugly black building, with a number of rectangular doors. . . . The outside looks so dirty that it is a relief to gain the interior which is as remarkable for its cleanly appearance, being painted throughout a light grey—gallery, pulpit, walls, and all except the pews. One would imagine it would be a relief to many a soul to escape from the close courts and dirty hovels in the neighbourhood of the chapel into its interior, where there is at least light and space. Doubtless it is so to some; but the congregation is not large, and as is the case with most city churches and chapels of all denominations, a considerable number of its members come from the suburbs to the place of worship in connection with which they have been brought up.

Anyone who follows our footsteps will notice, as we have done, the odd variety of pulpits. In the Lever Street chapel, that article resembles a huge goblet. The service is the ordinary dissenting one, consisting of hymns, extempore prayers and reading of the Scriptures. The hymn book used is John Wesley's, with several additions made by authority of the Annual Assembly. Before the commencement of the sermon, we were startled by the sudden appearance of an individual who, advancing to the front of the pews, mounted a form to read out a series of notices. The preacher supplemented one of these notices respecting the pleasure the stewards would have in letting seats or pews, by a few remarks, from which we gathered that considerable diffidence in renting the same was shown by a portion of the congregation.

While there is a leaning on the part of the Wesleyan Connexion towards the Anglican Church, the United Free Methodists have an equally observable tendency towards the system and principles of the Congregational body. Thus, at Lever Street, some of the people have a movement on foot to secure a pastor entirely for that chapel at least during the circuit term, and to discontinue contributing to the support of other chapels. If this is carried out, the main distinguishing feature between the two systems—Independent and Free Methodist—excepting class organization, will have begun to disappear; and even in the matter of class meetings, the discipline is growing much more lax, as shown by the fact that some of those in office do not attend these gatherings.

The sermons of the Manchester Free Methodists cannot be described as intensely spiritual; they are rather familiar exhortations relating to the common circumstances of life. They abound in warnings against many specially-named places of amusement, and deal largely in the temptations to which young people, particularly apprentices and servant girls, are subjected. As the bulk of the congregation is composed of the working classes, there is doubtless a special applicability about much of this preaching.

'A Wanderer', *Sketches of Methodism In Manchester* (1871), 15 f

(iv)   *A mining village*

It is to the chapel we are going—the gathering place for worship, the house of God. It is a plain, unpretentious building, commodious enough, but lacking both in beauty and comfort. In the pulpit is a tall, spare man, with a face in which mysticism and intelligence are strangely blended. We learn that he is a miner from a neighbouring colliery. . . . Never shall I forget the singing of that service. There was a little scraping and twanging of fiddle-strings before all the stringed instruments—of which there were a dozen—were brought into accord with the organ, but then such a glorious outburst of music as could not fail to help the spirit of devotion. How these North folks sing. . . .

We felt the Divine enchantment of the hour. The glory of the Lord was in His sanctuary. Forgotten in the ecstatic bliss of mystic communion with heaven were the bare, unsightly walls, the hard seats, the dreary pit. perhaps beneath our very feet, in which men crawl like beasts for six days in the week, heaving coals, naked to the waist, while the perspiration makes white channels down their grimy bodies; forgotten the hardship, the dull, aching monotony, and the familiar thought of death . . . the vision of God and the Celestial City are seen by these men in that outburst of song in which the soul was finding expression. . . . After the first hymn came the prayer. Prayer is not for criticism. When a man is talking with his Maker, he should be safe from the attacks of fault finders. But there are men who have what the old Methodists called the 'gift of prayer', and the preacher had that gift. . . . The pitman preacher talked with God with the familiarity which comes of frequent communion, and yet, withal, with a reverence that moved even the restless youths sitting near the pulpit. . . . And the preacher carried his congregation along on the strong pinions of his own faith, until a low rumbling of murmured responses broke forth in loud 'Amens'. Suddenly one man sprang to his feet, and, with a loud shout of 'Praise the Lord', jumped into the air. Few observed it, or if they observed it, took any notice, so absorbed were they in their own devotions. 'Make the place of Thy feet glorious,' exclaimed the preacher, and with outcries of 'He does it,' 'He does it now,' the petition came to a close. The reading of the Scriptures was interspersed with a few remarks here and there more or less appropriate—generally less—and the service would not have suffered by their omission. But the Sermon —who shall describe it? It was a Sermon to be heard, not to be reported. What a mixture of humour, passionate appeal, thrilling exhortations and apposite illustrations it was. . . . Laughter and tears this preacher commanded at will, and when he closed with heartsearching appeals to the unconverted to fly to the Cross for pardon, one almost wondered that men and women did not spring to their feet and rush somewhere —anywhere, exclaiming with Bunyan's Pilgrim, 'Life, Life, Eternal Life'!

The service was over, and, with the remembrance of that sermon as a life-long legacy, we retraced our steps homeward, stronger for having sat at the feet of this rugged Elijah of the coalpit, a hewer of coals for six days down in the deep dark mine, and a very flame of fire on the seventh.

Primitive Methodist Magazine (1896), 830–31

B Church discipline

(i) *A defence*

The discipline of the church is, in brief, a mutual contract for essential truth and for holiness. . . . Sinning brethren are to be first spoken with in private, then publicly, before the church; and, if after that, they will not hear, they are to be to us as heathen and publicans. Such is our Lord's law. Similarly among the Jews admonition was the first stage of discipline, and anathema, or exclusion, the last. . . .

The kindly wise treatment of excluded members is a lesson we still need to learn in modern times. . . .

Truth is seldom objectionable till it comes to be applied. So long as it is held in principle only, men are ready to commend it; but when it is pressed home upon themselves, or when it is found to condemn systems they have long known and cherished, they begin to regard it with suspicion. And thus it has fared with the truths we are now expounding. Nearly all churches started with the theory that membership is a privilege: that it is to be given to those only who have the appropriate character, and that for certain acts it may be withdrawn. And herein nearly all agree. But once apply the principle, and it becomes, in the judgment of many, tyranny or persecution, or uncharitableness. At best it is deemed impracticable.

All these forms the objections of opponents have assumed. *Tyranny*, however, it is not. Tyranny is the supremacy of mere will. The government of the church is the supremacy of the divine law. Tyranny and the supremacy of the law are, in truth, opposite terms. *Persecution* it is not; all secular penalties the church dis-owns. Church membership is no civil right; and *that* is all that Christian discipline witholds.

The other pleas deserve more consideration. Is it uncharitable? Is it impracticable?

It is maintained then that this system of affected purity is a denial of the rule laid down by our Lord. He tell us that the tares and the wheat are both to grow together till the harvest. An apostle still further enforces this precept by bidding men not to anticipate the decisions of the great day, and 'to judge nothing before the time'.

But is this the meaning of our Lord's parable, or of apostolic teaching? In our Lord's interpretation of the parable, He tells us that the field is *not the church, but the world*; and the command that bids us let both grow together, though a sufficient reason for not leading a heretic to the stake, is no reason for keeping him in nominally Christian fellowship. Elsewhere, moreover, he bids us tell our brother his fault, and if he refuse to hear us, we are to tell it to the church, and if he will not hear the church, he is to be to us as 'a heathen man and a publican'. . . . Clearly, while *some* judgment is forbidden, *other* judgment, and exclusion even, are enjoined.

Or the objection takes another form. The process is impracticable. Men cannot certainly decide, it is said, who are Christians, and is it not presumptuous to try? Better leave each man to his conscience and to God.

The objection is common and popular. It commends itself to many who accept it as much from humility as from any theory they have formed on the duty of the church. 'Our judgments are fallible', is their first principle; and it is as old as the hills. . . . But is this fallibility peculiar to the judgments we form of the religion of others? Do we cease to judge of a man's honesty because we have been deceived? Did an apostle cease to judge himself because compelled to say, 'I am conscious of no wrong, yet am I not thereby justified, for He that judgeth me is the Lord?' If men know not what true religion is, then indeed they may scruple to test the religion of others. But if they are themselves converted, they are bound to watch over one another, and unitedly to seek the salvation of the world. For both purposes they must judge. To forbid them to judge others is as absurd as to send medical men to visit infected districts, and to administer remedies indiscriminately, without allowing them to ask the symptoms of the disease they seek to heal, or even to ascertain, in any given case, whether the enforced patients are diseased at all.

J. Angus, *Christian Churches* (1862), 34–41

(ii) *The court of the church meeting*

1842. December 2nd. The pastor had understood several months ago
that Richard Martin had fallen into the sin from which it had been
hoped he had been fully recovered by the grace of God, the sin of
intemperance. Two of our brethren being called upon stated that some
weeks before they had been aware of his fall and had entreated him to
beware of its evils, but one of the deacons, having gone to his house on
that morning for the same purpose, being also called on, testified that
he found him in a state of inebriety accompanied by painful circumstances. Our pastor offered our earnest prayers for divine direction in
this solemn and distressing case; after which he gave it as his view that
we were required by regard to the honour of our Lord and to the
welfare and recovery of our fallen brother to exclude him from visible
connexion with the Christian church on earth. . . .

1844. July 17th. It is reported that Martha Smith has married a man
whom she does not herself consider a converted character and having
thereby acted contrary to divine command to come out from the
fellowship of the world, to be separate with respect to the marriage
relation, to marry only in the Lord, the church agrees in conscience
with their pastor to express their deep grief and solemn disapproval of
the step and would entreat that the Lord might grant unto her due
contrition and enable her to walk faithfully in the circumstances in
which she is placed. . . .

1844. October 2nd. Mrs Mary Hodgson had failed to be present at the
Lord's table for several months. . . .

1844. October 30th. The visitors reported to the Church that in
consequence of the violence of her husband's temper and treatment
towards her in respect of religion it was quite impossible for her to fill
up her place in the church for the present. After consideration it was
concluded that seeing her absence was not voluntary, she having been
so far as could be understood deceived as to the religious character of
her husband previous to marriage, and no party to her present separation from our Ordinances, it seems to be the duty of the church to retain
her on at least nominal fellowship until further development of divine
providence appear. . . .

1846. December 2nd. Mrs Jane Baldwin had fallen into gross sin and
which precluded the appointment of visitors. . . . She is excluded from
the church but our hope is expressed that the sense of her depredation
may be deepened, and that the humiliation which she manifests may be
matured into Godly sorrow and lead to her restoration. . . .

1857. December 3rd. It was reported that George Cowper had been obliged to stop payments . . . the church concludes to express their grief that they cannot acquit him of a depth of negligence and imprudence which has lead him near to what is dishonourable and untrustworthy of the scrupulous integrity of a Christian tradesman but do not consider that they have before them evidence of a kind to justify their doing otherwise than retaining him in their communion. . . .

> *The Minute Book of Pembroke Baptist Chapel, Liverpool,* in the Baptist Union Library, London

C   The Ministry

(i)   *Ministering to the new age*

The duties and toils, both of ministers and private Christians must always increase in proportion to the advancement of religion. The mere fact of constant accessions to the Church imposes on a Dissenting pastor an onerous and anxious duty, delightful indeed, but most imperative and impossible of being devolved upon others. This has, during the last thirty years, been felt in its full force, for most of the churches have greatly increased.

The disposition to decline three services, and to preach only in the morning and the evening of the Lord's Day, has been steadily gaining ground, but the more laborious preparation for the pulpit has increased in equal proportion, and the exposition of the Scriptures has become a general practice, by which the labour of the minister in his study is greatly augmented. Lectures on given subjects are become more frequent; and as these are designed to counteract infidelity, Popery or Socinianism, and are sometimes delivered on working days, they form a considerable tax on the minister's time, and on his strength, both physical and mental.

The increase of Sabbath Schools has diminished the labour of the pastor, who formerly spent much time in catechizing; but where he takes his due measure of interest in these schools, they make frequent calls on him to address both children and teachers, and to hold meetings as well as to preach sermons for their support. . . .

Foreign missions are now so closely associated with the Christian Church that almost every minister who is awake to his duty, spends some considerable portion of his life in cherishing auxiliary missionary societies. . . .

The New Marriage Act has brought an unexpected augmentation of labour on ministers. For, though the law admits of solemnizing marriage as a civil act, before the registrar alone, Dissenters are either not generally weaned from Popish ideas of marriage, or they think it so necessary to yield to popular prejudice, that many of our places of worship are registered for the marriage ceremony, and the ministers are generally requested to perform a religious service on this occasion. . . .

If, during the last age, preaching three times on the Lord's day has somewhat declined, the extra services for religious and benevolent societies are not the only modes in which the labours of ministers have been rendered equal to those of their predecessors; for the press has more generally been employed than in former eras. . . . Numerous are the treatises on every subject connected with religion and sacred literature, which attest the diligence of ministers, and their solicitude for the young, for the kingdom of Christ in the world, and for the defence of truth against errror in all its forms.

The support of the Dissenting ministry has varied but little during the last thirty years from the ratio of former periods. That support has always been scanty; and though Dissenters have recently increased their contributions to maintain the numerous benevolent institutions that have sprung up, the pastor who has not a large congregation or a private fortune, or some other source of income, must be much embarrassed in bringing up a family. . . .

As the character of the ministry marks that of the Church, Dissenters have, for the last thirty years, paid anxious attention to the piety, as well as the abilities of those they admit to the pastoral office. A person educated in an orthodox Dissenting College, must first have been admitted into a church as one born of God; and be recommended by the pastor and the flock as a man distinguished for piety and gifts, and a desire to be useful in the service of Christ. If during their studies any of them forfeit this character, they are expelled as unworthy of the ministry. Those who are chosen to the pastorate, hold their office during good behaviour, and cannot retain it with a stain on their characters. . . . Dissenting ministers are expected to be men of study, abstaining from worldly amusements and devoting themselves to the care of their flocks. A hunting, shooting or card-playing parson is not known, and would not be tolerated in any class of Evangelical Dissenters.

J. Bennett, *The History of Dissenters during the last thirty years 1808–38* (1839), 275–8, 302–3

(ii)   *The tyranny of the deacons*

It is my conviction that in many of our churches the pastor is depressed far below his just level. He is considered merely in the light of a speaking brother. He has no official distinction or authority. He may flatter like a sychophant, he may beg like a servant, he may woo like a lover, but he is not permitted to enjoin like a ruler. His opinion is received with no deference, his person treated with no respect; and in the presence of some of his lay tyrants, if he say anything at all, it must be somewhat similar to the ancient soothsayers, for he is only permitted to peep and mutter from the dust.

> J. A. James, *Church Members Guide* (2nd edn.,
> 1850), 60

What is the deacon of some of our dissenting communities? Not simply the laborious, indefatigable, tender-hearted dispenser of the bounty of the Church: the instructor of the poor: the comforter of the distressed. No, but the 'Bible of the minister', the patron of the living and the wolf of the flock; an individual who, thrusting himself into the seat of government, attempts to lord it over God's heritage, by dictating alike to the pastor and the members; who thinks that in virtue of his office, his opinion is to be law on all matters of Church government, whether temporal or spiritual; who, upon the least symptom of opposition to his will, frowns like a tyrant upon the spirit of rising rebellion amongst his slaves. This man is almost as distant from the deacon of apostolic times as the deacon of the Vatican. Such men there have been, whose spirit of divination in the Church has produced a kind of diaconophobia in the minds of many ministers who have suffered most woefully from their bite, and have been led to resolve to do without them altogether rather than be worried any more. Hence it is that, in some cases, the nonscriptural plan of committees has been resorted to, that the tyranny of the Lord Deacons might be avoided. These are rare cases in large towns, but they are much more frequent in remoter neighbourhoods. There is not a more browbeaten, abused and overborne set of men out of slavery than some of the Dissenting ministers in country places. They become the mere tools of one or two rich or well-to-do men, whose ignorance is only to be excelled by their arrogance.

> J. P. Mursell from a lecture entitled *Notice to
> Quit* given in the Free Trade Hall, Manchester,
> 12 January 1862

(iii) *The support of the good deacons*

My real mentor on the diaconate whose advice was generally sound, though over-cautious, was Philip le Gros, J.P., a man of culture and considerable wealth. He acted as a sort of brake when I was inclined to drive recklessly, putting his hand on my arm and saying quietly: 'Wait, my dear friend, wait ! The world comes round to him who waits.' It was excellent advice, particularly to a rather impetuous young minister.

One of the best deacons I ever had was William Bret Harvey, a chemist and stationer in Bath Street. He was the prime mover in temperance work and musical societies of various kinds. He acted as our unpaid organist and choir-leader, and was superintendent of the Sunday School. Affectionate, genial, and devout, he was universally beloved.

My chief friend in Frome was Joseph Tanner, a man about my own age, possessed of great shrewdness and business ability. Just before my settlement in the town, he had entered into partnership with another deacon of Zion, Mr T. Butler, who had a small printing business and published the *Somerset and Wilts Journal*. Tanner's ability combined with Butler's knowledge of printing speedily developed the business, and today the firm of 'Butler & Tanner' has a world-wide reputation for good work produced under the best conditions.

These are samples of the men whom I had about me in my first pastorate, to whom I owed much for any discipline of character and success in work subsequently gained. And I could pay a similar tribute to the Christian womanhood of that church.

> An Independent Parson, Autobiography of Dr
> Alfred Rowland (1923), 61-2, concerning his
> pastorate at Frome 1865-75

Among the men who welcomed Mr Clifford to Praed Street were Joseph Morgan, whom he described as 'true as steel, tender as a mother', Edward Brown, the Secretary, 'quiet, genial, poetry-loving', and Thomas Poynton Dexter, 'one of the three deacons when I accepted the pastorate, and he soon became a cherished friend, a helpful companion and a welcome comrade'. All through his ministry we shall discover that he put unstinted trust in his deacons, who reciprocated with affectionate loyalty. The young pastor and Mr Dexter spent their Saturday afternoons in reading the Latin Classics together and discussing questions of literature, philosophy and politics. So friendships were

cemented that lasted through the years. 'Never at any time,' says Dr
Clifford, 'have I had any trouble with church officers or people,
excepting such as have arisen from what I call the "tyranny of their
love". My debt to my Deacons is immeasurable.'

> Sir James Marchant, *Dr John Clifford* (1924),
> 39–40, concerning his arrival at Praed Street
> in 1858

(iv) *Ministerial pretensions*
(*Mr Paterson, the Dissenting Lecturer, speaks*)
'I am utterly sick of the way in which some of our men conduct
themselves, it is so wanting in every feature of moral dignity, and so
calculated to bring our principles into contempt. . . . Some of our men
. . . no sooner put themselves into long coats and soft hats than they
strut about as if they ought to have been vicars and deans. . . . If they
don't succeed, they blame the deacons, men who gratuitously devote
all they are and have to the cause of Christ; if they don't feel comfortable, they charge their discontents upon the deacons, and ask con-
temptuously what can be expected from butchers and bakers and
candlestick makers, as if Nonconformist ministers themselves did not
come from the middle classes of the country. The fact is we had better
accept the disagreeable conclusion that half-hearted men must either
go from us or be put away. They must be got rid of.'

> J. Parker, *Weaver Stephen* (1886), 31

(v) *A crisis*
Much of the old, vigorous eloquence was strong in its effects, because
designedly adapted to a rough, uncultured audience. The spread of
popular education and the cultivation of discriminating taste have
rendered some of the old pulpit devices hopelessly inappropriate to
modern hearers. Of course, this can not be said of a really great orator
such as Robert Hall, whose style was as perfect from a literary point of
view as it was effective in popular influence. But another consideration
must be added. The older generation of preachers took it for granted
that their people had no doubts concerning the great doctrines with
which they dealt; and, for the most part, they were right in their assum-
tion. . . . So well established was the verbal authority of the Bible
that the preacher had but to quote a text to determine a controversy.
This gave him an immense advantage, and contributed enormously to
the effectiveness of his pulpit eloquence.

The *Evangelical Magazine* for January 1800 contains an extract from the diary of a minister who, having heard the celebrated Church of England clergyman, Romaine, preach at Blackfriars in the year 1794, makes the following comment: 'The sermon was short and good, but without much order or method. The people were very attentive, and to all appearance much affected and comforted. I observed that he did not attempt to *prove* anything, but took all his doctrines for granted.' An awakening of the restless spirit of enquiry began early in the century. Jay of Bath referred to it in the address that he gave at his own ordination, saying, 'A disposition for novelty in religious truth is the spring of error running through the flowery field of speculation into the gulf of apostasy.' That there were some who had already moved from the old standard of Gospel preaching is suggested by Jay's remarks in his confession of belief, where he says: 'the doctrine of the Atonement, not in a reserved, ambiguous way, in which many use the terms when denying them, but "Christ dying for our sins", in the proper sense of the expression, I consider as that which constitutes the good news or glad tidings which the Gospel signifies'. The context would suggest that the people whose ideas he is repudiating are the Unitarians. There is little or no evidence that such views had as yet found a lodgement in orthodox congregations.

How entirely different is the situation we see about us today! It is not only that education has encouraged the congregation to make heavier demands on the preacher. The age is critical. A spirit of enquiry is in the air. People are no longer content to sit under their minister; some of them are more ready to sit upon him. The old authority of the pulpit has disappeared. Round assertions count for little. The preacher must 'prove all things'. Nor will his hearers be satisfied with mere 'proof-texts', however long an array of them he may have marshalled. He must show his teaching to be what they reckon 'reasonable', or they will have none of it. . . .

At about the middle of the century preaching began to enlarge its scope and range itself over a wider field. The earlier generation had shrunk from speculation as dangerously suggestive of heresy. But the stirring of new thought in the community could not but affect the pulpit. For a while the preacher seemed to lag behind his congregation, and thinking men began to complain of the 'pulpit platitudes' with which their intelligence was insulted. Gradually the crust of caution broke up and fresh thoughts welled through. Then we had the spectacle of the younger ministry—especially in the Nonconformist churches— forging ahead in advance of their people, sometimes to the dismay of sober-minded deacons. Various speculative questions came to be discussed in the pulpit, such as Evolution, Future Punishment, theories of the Atonement. It must be confessed that this was not infrequently done in the crudest fashion by men but ill-equipped for the difficult tasks they had undertaken. Simple people came to gather very confused notions of the discussions they heard of for the first time in their young pastor's sermons, and the immediate results were not altogether satisfactory. But this is inevitable in times of transition. Probably the same thing happened during the Reformation at the hands of indiscreet half-educated Protestant preachers. It was unsettling; but though it is uncomfortable to feel unsettled, it may not be altogether unwholesome if only the rude awakening leads to a wider settlement in the end. At all events, a ferment of fresh ideas was excited, and the dull torpor to which most minds gravitate was broken up and enlivened with some glimmering of thought. If only it could be rightly directed, that should be a beginning of better things.

> W. F. Adeney: *A Century's Progress* (1901),
> 192–4, 205–7

D Connexionalism

This year is the Jubilee year of the Congregational Union of England and Wales. Its beginning was small, but now its power is great. Some few feared then that it would deprive the Churches of their independency, and that the end would be to transfer all the power of the denomination to some central committee. The phantom of centralization frightened men then as it does now. But after fifty years' experience, is there a Church in the denomination that will stand up and say that the Union has deprived it of its liberty, or interfered with its independency? If there is, let it speak out boldly. I know that there are ignorant men who make a ghost of this to terrify themselves. I know that there are wicked men who are bent on doing mischief under the cloak of caring for Independency, who beguile innocent men to believe that the Congregational Union and every other union are in league to deprive the Churches of their liberty, and transfer all power to their committees and organisations; but where is the Church that will stand up and testify that the Congregational Union has in any way interfered with its independency? It has in many ways assisted the Churches, and proved itself invaluable to religion. How many societies have sprung out of the Union which have greatly benefitted the

Churches? How many chapels have received help from the Chapel Building Societies of the denomination, for which the Union has done so much? Who can tell the service that the Pastors' Retiring Fund has done to the Churches of our denomination? And what would have become of this fund had it not been for the Union? The Union has never interfered with the liberty and independency of any Church, but it has done an immense good in assisting the Churches and cheering their pastors. What is true of the Congregational Union is true of all other Unions, small and large, although their power for good is not so great, but in their relation to the liberties of the Church they are quite as faithful. The strength of Congregationalism is in its power to secure cooperation in perfect consistency with the liberty of the Churches. . . . Our denomination in England and Wales has more than doubled during the last fifty years; and more practical work has been done during that period, than in all the previous history of our Churches; and how could all this be done without some union for consultation and cooperation? The most delusive cry that ever was raised in a denomination is the cry that there is a danger to the independency of the Churches in the unions formed. The whole thing is only an attempt to blindfold the simple and the ignorant.

From an address by the Reverend Dr J. Thomas, *The Jubilee Proceedings of the Congregational Union of England and Wales* (1882), 105

E The Sacraments

(i) *The Lord's supper: a feeble apologetic*

Definition. A Sacrament is a divine institution, of universal obligation, for conveying to the mind and feelings of men, by some sensible substance and symbolical action, an impressive idea of the most essential blessings of redemption by the Messiah. . . .

They are signs *confirmatory* of divine truths and promises: and *instructive*, especially to men of inferior cultivation. . . .

The Lord's Supper is,

1. A *religious festival*: generically resembling the sacrifice—feasts of the heathen (derived, no doubt, from a pure fountain of primeval Divine instruction), and of the worshippers of the true God.

2. *Instituted by Christ* The different phraseology of our Lord, in the accounts of Matthew, Mark, Luke and Paul, is to be resolved into the

fact of our Lord's saying the predicates, at different times, during the celebration.

3. *Commemorative.* As irrefragable evidence of the great fact.

4. *Significant ex instituto:* of,

   (i) The spiritual life by the death of Christ produced and sustained
   (ii) Union to Christ, in receiving Him as Sovereign, Saviour and Teacher—rejecting all false religions—acknowledging His people as our brethren—binding ourselves by solemn covenant engagements. . . .

On the qualifications of communicants.

These must be such as belong to the idea of 'remembering' Christ; such a remembrance of Him as *he intended*—holy, spiritual, devoted. (Was Judas present at the institution?—no.)

Preparation: not anxious, superstitious, mechanical, but the habitual frame of heart. Yet especial devotion, when practicable, is highly conducive to edifying. . . . Supposing a real presence—what would be the benefit of it? Redemption and grace do not act mechanically or physically. Suppose the penitent malefactor had asked for some of the blood of Jesus, to sprinkle himself with—or to drink it—or to have some portion of the lacerated flesh, to bite, chew and swallow!—*Cannibalism.*

[V. John vi. 63: 2 Cor. v. 16: M. de Feliche's Letters, no. xii: Campbell's *British Banner*, 20 December, 1848.]

       J. Pye Smith, *First Lines of Christian Theology*
       (1854), 654–5, 674–5, 677

(ii) *The Lord's supper: high sacramentalism*

In the eagerness with which Protestant controversialists have maintained that the Bread and the Wine are only symbols it has been forgotten that if they are symbols they symbolize something. Such exaggerated attention has been concentrated on the visible signs, the truth has been reiterated with such earnestness that signs are only signs, that we have come to think that the service has no spiritual value. It is time that we remembered Who it was that instituted the Rite, and what He Himself said when he distributed the Elements.

If it had been instituted by ourselves to commemorate Christ, the whole service and not the elements alone would have been merely symbolic. To recur to the old illustration: if a soldier in the ranks of a besieging army hands a key to his own general, the *act* is symbolic as well as the *key*. It is simply the expression of the confidence and hope of a man having no authority to surrender the city, that the city will soon be taken. It is a mere dramatic ceremony. We can imagine circumstances in which it would be very effective—circumstances in which it would stir the courage and fire the ardour of those who have become weary of the seige; but its whole value and force would lie in its effect upon the imaginations and emotions of those who witnessed it. But when the governor of the city does the same thing, the act is a mere dramatic ceremony no longer. Its value does not lie in the impressiveness and scenic solemnity with which it may be accepted. It represents a real transfer of power. And so when Christ gives us Bread, and says, 'This is My Body', it is not mere dramatic ceremony, deriving all its worth from its 'didactic' meaning or its 'impressive' power. His Body is actually given. 'The Bread which we break' is 'the Communion of the Body of Christ.' 'The cup of blessing which we bless' is 'the Communion of the Blood of Christ.' The Elements are the key surrendering possession of the city: the book conferring his dignity on the abbot; the staff transferring authority to the bishop; the ring ratifying the vow of marriage; the 'seal', to use the language of our fathers, of the covenant of grace.

> R. W. Dale, 'The Doctrine of the Real Presence and the Lord's Supper' in H. R. Reynolds (ed.), *Ecclesia*, 1st series (1870), 315 f

(iii) *Believers' baptism: a simple literalism*

In not baptizing babies, Baptists follow the example of the apostles and those disciples who were associated with them. There is no mention of the baptism of babies in the New Testament, nor in any extant works of Christians of the second century. . . .

Baptism is for believers. It follows discipleship. 'Make disciples of all nations, baptizing them into the name of the Father, and of the Son and of the Holy Spirit'. The disciples were made first, and afterwards baptized. With this agrees what is said about the rumour which reached the Pharisees early in the ministry of Jesus, 'that Jesus was making and baptizing more disciples than John (although Jesus Himself baptized not, but His disciples)'. On the day of Pentecost 'they that received' Peter's word 'were baptized'. All the references to baptism in the book of the Acts of the Apostles are to the same effect. . . .

Baptists dare not alter a divine ordinance. To them it seems as if those who call infant sprinkling Christian baptism teach us for their doctrine of baptism 'the precepts of men', 'leave the commandments of God, and hold fast' human tradition. The result is that they 'reject the commandment of God', the baptism of believers, that they may 'keep their tradition', infant sprinkling. In Christendom today the order is not that which Christ prescribed, 'make disciples', and baptize them. There is no baptism in sprinkling, and the sprinkling precedes instead of follows discipleship. . . .

Baptists . . . cannot, without doing violence to their own principles, ascribe to Baptism any cleansing efficacy or regenerating influence or saving grace. Asking evidence of contrition on account of sin, and some few signs of a change of heart and of discipleship to the Lord Jesus, as the condition precedent to baptism, they effectually guard the ordinance from exaggeration. Before they baptize candidates, the candidates are held to be 'members of Christ' and 'the children of God by the faith that is in Christ Jesus'. Professedly regenerated and redeemed, converted and made disciples before baptism, it is impossible that candidates should fall into the error that baptism regenerates or redeems converts or disciples, or even assists in or perfects the process by which 'a child of wrath' is made an 'heir of glory'. And thus the belief of Baptists keeps baptism in the place assigned to it by the Lord Jesus. On the other hand, the principle of unreserved loyalty to Christ . . . will not permit them to slight or neglect the ordinance. Seeing that Christ commanded that disciples should be baptized, and that apostles, acting under the great commission, baptized all who professed discipleship, Baptists consider that obedience is due to this commandment of Christ. It would be disloyal in their part not to obey.

C. Williams, *The Principles and Practices of the Baptists* (1879), 9–12, 20

(iv)   Believers' baptism: in the light of cosmic evolution

In two conspicuous particulars our world is different from that old world in which our fathers lived. We have seen born, grow, flourish a literary criticism of the Bible. What has that done for us? It has made the Bible more real, more precious in the deepest sense, more true, its men and women, realer flesh and blood, human brain and immortal spirit than ever before. It is more emphatically a true Book, it is more vitally the Book of God. For our teachers, who are experts, and for us who are only students, literary criticism of the Bible has made us understand our Bible better and love it more.

We have seen born, grow, flourish a new philosophy of the universe. We have adopted an evidence and authority which seem acceptable to our reason, the evolutionary account of the 'becoming' of things. And with what results? Why, that instead of looking for a lonely solitary God, who sits outside the Universe, watching it go, we have found a God immanent in all things, in all life, a God around us, who is the life of all things, in whom we live and move and have our being. This God has Jesus taught us to call Father, and he who seeks Him finds.

Nothing has happened to make this God less real, less sure.

Then, that which has been the inspiration of heroic lives, their strength, their hope, their comfort, their joy; is it not worth having now? Trouble will come. Sorrow will strike. Strength will ebb. The hour of loneliness and darkness waits. These men whom I have named ['our fathers'] and millions more, have indisputably found somewhere, somehow, strength and comfort, inspiration and hope. Is it no longer worth possessing? . . .

Strength is not to be discovered in a flash in the moment when trouble comes. It has to be accumulated beforehand. . . . It is our yesterdays which empty themselves into our today. In youth, young manhood, robust maturity, we have laid hold on God. In the hour of our need He keeps His loving hold on us. Learn the lesson, dear ones! Today, ask, and it shall be given you; seek and ye shall find, knock and it shall be opened unto you.

Of this splendid faith, the ordinance of Baptism which we are about to observe is the symbol and the pledge. To see this rite as Jesus saw it, no act of human life could be more solemn, none greater, none fraught with mightier meaning for the soul. With these words upon our lips, we go down into the Baptismal waters, 'Lord, into thine hand I commend my spirit', with these upon our heart we rise to walk in newness of life. It is not for death but for life we speak them, not from the depths of despair but from the heights of vison, rapture, consecration. With the glorious company of the Apostles, the goodly fellowship of the Prophets, the noble army of Martyrs, we commend our spirits to God. Yet our steps do not lead to torture, the scaffold or the stake, nor are our eyes closing in death. No: but in strength and hope and joy, in the power and pride of life, with work to do for men and praise to win from God, with free minds to serve Him and warm hearts to love Him, we speak the old heroic vow, 'Lord into thine hand I commend my spirit'.

C. F. Aked, *The Courage of the Coward* (n.d.),
94–8

F   The spirit of early nineteenth-century Wesleyanism

Letter of John Stephens, Superintendent of the Manchester Circuit to Jabez Bunting

Manchester February 1st 1821

My Dear Sir,

. . . I should be happy to give you an account of our affairs since the last Conference; but I have been so much personally concerned in them, that such a history from me would savour of too much egotism.

You will be pleased however to excuse a few observations, without putting such a construction upon them; especially when I assure you, that, if no Superintendent was ever placed in a more trying situation, none was ever more cordially, steadily or efficiently supported; and that if any plans have been adopted with wisdom and advantage the Connexion is more indebted to my excellent colleagues and to the sound part of this society than to your humble servant.

The objects we have kept in view are, 1st, to give the sound part of this society a decided ascendancy. 2. So to put down the opposition as to disable them from doing mischief. 3. To cure those of them who are worth saving. 4. To take the rest one by one and crush them when they notoriously commit themselves. The plan is likely to succeed. They are completely at our mercy. We have no long speeches; no moving and seconding wild and absurd resolutions; not a soul of them ventures to propose anything without first consulting me and obtaining my consent. A few of the ring-leaders have taken the sulks, and seldom attend our meetings; but for this we are not sorry. We have peace; we meet and do our business; and part like men of God. They are down, and we intend to keep them down. That they are not annihilated is rather for want of will than power; we wish to be careful in rooting up the tares (lest?), we should root up the wheat also. (The) poor people are getting better wages. Provisions are cheap. Their leaders have deceived them in their promises of revolution. They are growing tired of radicalism, and as that dies, religion will revive.

Our Congregations are good. Methodism stands high among the respectable people. We have had some awakenings and conversions. Nearly every seat is let in the New Chapel. The prayers are well attended. Much good is done there, and I feel the building of that Chapel, the introduction of the Liturgy, in our present success and future prospects in that part of the town, a reward for all I have suffered in Manchester. . . .

We have been very quiet here on the Queen's business. Though no men had stronger temptation, yet not one of us has lowered the dignity of the Christian pulpit by mixing up her name with the public Worship; and our numerous congregations prove that such cringing to a wicked faction was unnecessary anywhere. We feel justly offended at the conduct of some of our brethren in that respect. Please to tell me a little connexion news. Love to Mrs B. and all friends. Write soon— God bless you!

Yours truly,
J. Stephens
From J. Bunting's Correspondence, Methodist
Archives and Research Centre, London

G   The Nonconformist reaction

Talk of Rome! The Wesleyan Conference during the last three years has displayed a spirit of persecution which the Church of Rome would not have dared to exhibit in this country. Had the priesthood of that Church ventured in the present day to treat its members in this kingdom with the same remorseless tyranny as the Wesleyan Conference has manifested towards the Wesleyan laity, they would have provoked a civil war. To secure *unity* and *uniformity*, the ruling party in the Wesleyan Conference have adopted the very principles and means employed by the Papacy in purely popish countries—the only difference being that they have been 'intensified in their evils, and vulgarized in their manifestations by the lower and less cultivated condition of the class of men who have employed them'. The unprincipled oligarchy to which I have referred, having usurped to itself all the legislative, executive, judicial and administrative functions of the body, sets up its *will* as the rule and duty both for the preachers and the societies, while its indulgence is made the only source of their freedom. It has created and multiplied offices of honour and emolument, and grasped the patronage and profit of them all. It has usurped the appointment of all meetings—the election of all Committees—the nomination of all Chairmen —who are always men of the clerical order, investing them with power to prescribe or annul the deliberations of the Community at their pleasure—and to insist upon their complete subjection to pastoral authority. It has taken possession of all the connexional property, and the control of all connexional funds. It has converted its courts into inquisitions, its ministers into spies; and offered promotion to those who, for the good of the Church, would betray their dearest friends. It has re-established the odious system of tests, and questioning by penalty; and made it a crime worthy of excommunication for any of its jurors or judges to keep a conscience, to talk of mercy, or to acquit an independent man. It has anathematized the press, defied public opinion, and created barriers to oppose the spirit of progress and intelligence. Its legislation has been characterized by intense meanness, selfishness and craft. It first goads its victims to resistance, and then expels them for contumacy.

Principles so odious and claims so tyrannical are fatal to intelligence, progress and freedom. There can be no question that, had the Wesleyan Conference been 'invested with the absolute power which Rome once possessed', it would have 'equalled Rome itself in the spirit of persecution'. Had such been the case, your Lordship would not have escaped by simply answering the interrogatives of an impertinent young man at Leeds; you would certainly have been dragged to the bar of the Wesleyan Inquisition, and probably transferred to some cold apartment in the Tower, or to a warmer place in Smithfield.

To overturn and annihilate this system of priestly despotism, is the mission and purpose of the Wesleyan Reform, movement and of

Your Lordship's

Very obedient servant

W. Martin.

W. Martin, *Priestly Despotism Rampant in the Wesleyan Conference. A Letter to the Rt. Hon. Lord John Russell* (London, 1853), 87–8

H   Response to Catholicism

(i)   I lately visited a church in which there was more of awe, more of submission in humiliation than ever I have seen in any Independent, Baptist or Methodist congregation. There was kneeling in the aisle before the altar, there was covering of the face and eyes, there was silence, save for the solemn tolling of the bell, while the 'host' was elevated. There was every outward sign of earnest, prayerful feeling. Coming home, I asked myself, 'Does this, or does it not, put us to shame?' I felt that in some respects it does. It would be well if some

congregations had more of that 'decency and order' which we all
wish to cultivate.'

Reverend John Curwen in *The Congregational
Year Book* for 1871, 102

(ii)   Instead of long prayers, we should have a good many short ones.
And instead of being dependant on the 'frame of mind' (whatever that
may mean) that the minister is in, a large portion of the Prayers should
be printed, with responses for the congregation to repeat at very short
intervals. If it be objected that this would be a liturgy, I, of course, at
once reply—'Yes, I am in favour of liturgical help in our worship, not
by any means to the entire exclusion of extempore prayer, but for the
expression of all common wants, confessions, thanksgivings and peti-
tions. I would go even farther—most of our religious Countrymen love
the Liturgy of the Church of England and would use that.

'Layman' in *The Nonconformist and Independent,* 6 April 1882

(iii)   The great wave of Catholic sentiment which has been sweeping
over the Established Church during the last fifty years has sensibly
cast its spray upon the Nonconformist bodies of the country. Not
only in more stately structures for public worship, and in more ornate
services, can we recognize the influence of the Oxford movement
among the 'free churches', but even the doctrinal position of the latter
has in some respects moved nearer to that of the High Church party.

Editorial in *The Christian World*, 3 August
1882

(iv)   The truth is, that, in the word Ritualism, there is involved much
more than the popular mind seems to suppose. The present movement
in favour of ritual is not confined to ritualists, neither is it confined even
to Churchmen. It has been, when all things are considered, quite as
remarkable among Nonconformists and Presbyterians; not because
they have as much of it, but because they formerly had none, and
because their system appeared to have been devised and adjusted in
order to prevent its introduction, and to fix upon it even *in limine* the
aspect of a flagrant departure from first principles. Crosses on the outside of chapels, organs within them, rich pointed architecture, that

flagrant piece of symbolism, the steeple, windows filled with subjects in stained glass, elaborate chanting, the use of the Lord's prayer, which is no more than the thin end of the wedge that is to introduce fixed forms, and the partial movements in favour of such forms already developed, are among the signs which, taken all together, form a group of phenomena evidently referable to some cause far more deep and wide-working than mere servile imitation, or the fashion of the day. In the case of the organ, be it recollected that many who form part of the *crême de la crême* of Protestantism have now begun to use that which the Pope does not hear in his own Chapel or his sublime Basilica, and which the entire Eastern Church has ever shrunk from employing in its services.

With this I will mention a familiar matter, though it may provoke a smile. It is the matter of clerical costume; on which I will not scruple to say that, in my judgment, the party of costume is right. A costume for the clergy is as much connected with discipline and self-respect as an uniform for the army, and is no small guarantee for conduct. The disuse of clerical costume was a recent innovation; but thirty-five or forty years ago the abuse had become almost universal. It was consummated by the change in lay fashions—a very singular one—to a nearly exclusive use by men of black. The reaction began in the cut of the waistcoat, which, as worn by the innovators, was buttoned all the way up to the cravat. This was deemed so distinctly Popish, that it acquired the nickname of 'The Mark of the Beast'; and it is a fact that, among the tailors of the west-end of London, this shape of waistcoat was familiarly known as 'the M.B. waistcoat'. Any one who will now take the pains to notice the dress of the regular Presbyterian or Dissenting minister will, I think, find that, in a great majority of instances, he too, when in his best, wears, like the clergyman, the M.B. waistcoat.

W. E. Gladstone, *The Church of England and Ritualism* (1876), Advertisement (i.e. Preface)

3

NONCONFORMITY AND SOCIETY

As Nonconformity advanced from the lowly status of 'the Dissenting interest' to a position of numerical parity with the Established church, so confidence and self-assurance, and even smugness, attended its progress. One mark of this assurance was the willingness, and perhaps the necessity for Nonconformity to develop an articulated view of society and its problems, which in its turn reveals the extent to which these groups were themselves shaped by the culture and conditions of the century (**A** and **B**). In describing these relationships, care must be exercised to avoid caricature: *some* Dissenters, possibly the majority, especially of middle-class Congregationalists, submitted gladly to what Lovell Cocks has called 'the Babylonish captivity to individualistic laissez-faire' whilst remaining 'completely unconscious of its chains'. The editor of the *Nonconformist* in 1843 makes the view of that periodical quite clear (**C**(i)) as he had also done the year previously in publishing Herbert Spencer's youthful contributions on 'The Proper Sphere of Government'. There was however, an older Nonconformist individualism, which, predating the influence of the Utilitarians, was far more generous in its social sentiments, for it was the product of a continuing radical tradition within the congregations themselves, not an alien importation, leading necessarily to social attitudes very different from those of Miall and Spencer. Robert Hall, Leicestershire Baptist and radical politician, witnesses to a theme which reappeared in many different guises throughout the century (**C**(ii)). But whatever the nature of Dissenting individualism, to an enraged Anglican like Mr Robert Masheder, a Cambridge don, it spelt Political Dissent and therefore democracy, and so was wholly bad (**D**).

Within the Nonconformist tradition, however, the individualistic emphasis upon conversion had always to be held in tension with a corporate understanding of the church: as the normative social philosophy of Victorian England changed from individualism to collectivism, so correspondingly this second emphasis, which for much of the century was neglected, came into new prominence. Social Science (**E**) may well have been a middle-class fad of the mid-century, but at the same time it served especially when conjoined with the kingdom of God theology of the Christian Socialists as an important link between the 'Political Dissent' of the '30s and '40s and the 'Nonconformist conscience' or 'social gospel' of the '80s and '90s.

Other social pressures forced Dissenting congregations to institutionalize themselves in many novel ways throughout the century. The temperance movement, perhaps the most conspicuous of these, is illustrated by first a curious episode from pre-temperance days (**F**(i)) followed by two not untypical examples of early Dissenting temperance propaganda, the first logical and well-reasoned, the second a remarkable example of Wesleyan ethics, put to the service of the social aggression of the employing classes, and the social conditioning of the poor (**F**(ii)and (iii)). When however it came to prohibitory legislation, the old Dissenting fears of government might well militate against their most cherished schemes of social amelioration (**F**(iv)), though a hymn of Mrs Cheats underlines the fact that intemperance was a serious social problem, that its enemies *could* be genuine idealists and subsume their temperance propaganda into a wider vision of social justice (**F**(v)).

The Friendly Society was another of the institutions of the early Victorian chapel, sometimes, apart from the Sunday school, the only one (**H**(i)) and from this the institutional church of the later period was to develop. The two extracts on the basis and character of the Victorian Sunday school underline both why the school assumed such significance in the eyes of its lay supporters, and how it could be almost an autonomous religious republic within a congregation, having an independent existence of its own, and being responsible within Wesleyanism for many of the internal movements of revolt which resulted in the formation of the Methodist sects (**H**(ii) and (iii)).

Other groups also learned the importance of combination and corporate awareness and to them Nonconformity made a generous response: its contribution to the Trade Union movement, especially the contribution of Methodists to the Miners' and Agricultural Labourers' Unions, is not to be despised even though the extent of this is currently disputed. Even the most respectable organ of Dissent could not fail to applaud the logic of Joseph Arch's endeavours, though its enthusiasm seems partly to arise out of a wish to manipulate the situation against the old foe of the landed Anglican establishment (**I**).

This is not to say that Nonconformity's sympathies rested upon calculation alone. Nonconformist attitudes to the poor are illustrated from the pens of those who patronized them, those who preached to them and from those amongst the poor who discovered in the Nonconformist pulpit a means for calling their colleagues to self-realization (**J**(i–v)). Nor is this simply a theme domestic to Nonconformity: that Andrew Mearns, William Booth and Charles Booth were all Nonconformists is itself significant, but a final extract (**J**(vi)) indicates how vulnerable Dissenters were to the cant of philanthropy divorced from a real sense of social justice.

The horizon of concern was not narrowly confined to domestic issues: long debated was the tension between the need to submit to the state's military demands and the equal duty to display a pacifist conscience. Henry Richard MP, the loudest Victorian spokesman for internationalism, had clear views as to how the tension should be resolved which failed to convince many of his fellow religionists, many of whom in the last two decades of the century became caught up with the social imperialism of Joseph Chamberlain, himself a Birmingham Unitarian (**K**(i)). An even more crucial breaking point in Nonconformity's social attitudes was similarly an imperial concern, the future of Ireland. The story of how the Parnell affair led to the coining of the phrase 'the Nonconformist conscience' is well known though the nature of the conscience has been much debated in recent years. All too easily it could lapse into an unlovely onslaught from a determined, Puritanical, middle-class sectarianism against the drink, gambling and thriftlessness of the classes below and above it to the ignoring of the deeper social problems which afflicted the nation (**L**).

But if the 'Nonconformist conscience' was at least in part the outcome of Miall's definition of individualism, the 'social gospel' was in some measure a child of Robert Hall's more positive concern for the individual, and stands as a proper, practical and involved corrective to the implicit pietism of the tradition of conscientious separation, though it of course could easily lapse into something little better than a vague evolutionary meliorism. Two Baptists illustrate the flowering of the social gospel in late Victorian Nonconformity; a college principal argues from the book of Exodus at one and the same time the fatal consequences of sin and the limiting impact of environment upon human life, and one of the great princes of the pulpit argues in a Fabian Tract the consonance of Christianity and collectivism (**M** and **N**).

A   Self-awareness

Commerce and manufacturers have done more towards realizing that needy ascendancy (of true religion) during the last two centuries, than has been done by feudalism during the thousand years preceding. The effect of those forms of industry in giving to the Christianity of Europe a greater degree of purity and power, and the degree in which they have contributed to bring the other continents of the globe into connection with Europe, exhibit a grand preliminary movement, the results of which will no doubt have their place among the great facts pertaining to the later history of our species.

The United States and the colonial empire of Great Britain have been called into existence during the interval mentioned, and mainly as the effect of commercial industry.

With this great fact in the history of modern Europe, we might connect a multitude of lesser facts as they present themselves in different localities, all tending to the same conclusion. Indeed, so far is it from being the nature of the system of manufactures to render men indifferent to religion, that where that system obtains, much more is manifestly done to uphold and diffuse religion than is done in neighbourhoods of a different description. It is found in such places, that the edifices raised both by the state and by the more wealthy of the land for public worship, are not so numerous as are those which owe their existence to the voluntary effort of the people themselves. Some of the people in such districts—at times considerable portions of them—may suffer themselves to be ensnared by the artifices of designing men; but the religious statistics both of England and Scotland show that the religious feeling is nowhere so powerful as in the places where large bodies of men are brought together for purposes of handicraft and trade. . . .

Now this habit (of industry), so effective in its influence on the communities of the earth, is exacted in the gospel from all who would be numbered among its disciples. It does not enjoin the rich so to care for the poor, as to supersede the necessity of that industry which should ever be allied with a state of need; nor does it so press the hopes of a future and better state of being upon the believer, as to disqualify him for wordly enterprise and exertion. All our duties in relation to each other are inculcated so as to harmonize with a pervading spirit of activity; and all the felicities we hope to realize in the future are made to blend with the obligations under which we are placed in regard to the present. Its command is that, 'if any man will not work, neither shall he eat'; and it teaches, explicitly, that those who substitute the habits of the idler and the busybody, 'working not at all', for those of industry, are persons who should be put away from Christian fellowship as walking disorderly (2 Thess. chap. iii). Its clear expectation is that those who profess to be Christians should know how to unite 'diligence in business' with 'fervour in spirit, concerning the Lord'. Thus industry, in place of being merely a social virtue, inculcated on the principles of human wisdom or inexpediency, is made to be indispensable, in the great majority of mankind, to religious consistency, and is enforced, accordingly, by the highest possible sanctions.

In consonance with these views, it is found, that in these later ages, the commercial ingenuity and enterprise of the world have their place, for the most part, among Christian nations, and, since the Reformation, among those states of Christendom professing the faith of the Gospel in its purer form. In the history of Germany, of France, of Holland, of Britain, and of the United States, we have ample illustration of the connection which subsists between a pure Christianity and habits of industry—and, in consequence, between a pure Christianity and the wealth, power, culture and happiness of nations.

R. Vaughan, *The Age of Great Cities* (1843),
312–14, 319–20, 358–60

B   Self-assurance

'Dissent in the present day is increasing as a political engine.' . . .
There was a time when to name a man a Dissenter was, in certain
circles, equivalent to calling him a heretic of the first degree. With the
lapse of years the term, as it became better and more generally understood, continued to lose much of its opprobriousness. In our day the
word 'political' must be tacked on to the old term, in order to describe
a very bad species of the race. To call by bad names is a low, spiteful
and childish method of attack, but it is done in respect to us, and we
must bear the nickname in the best possible temper, until the time
comes when want of information will not make our Episcopalian
friends judge us hybrids sprung from monsters because our convictions
on matters affecting the well-being of the Church of Christ differ from
their own. . . . The people, particularly in our large towns, where
Dissent flourishes most luxuriantly, are daily advancing in general
information. In common with the knowledge of matters belonging to
social life, they are gaining acquaintance with the nature and obligations of citizenship and government. In proportion to the increase of
information are they impressed with the conviction of increased and
multiplied obligations. The consciousness of these new obligations
affects their actions, when they are called upon to exercise civil functions, some of which functions the government declares they *must*
execute, under a penalty for not doing so. For which performance are
the Dissenters called 'political'—for fulfilling the duties which the ruling
power makes imperative, or for attending to those which common
sense and the feeling of manhood teach them to fulfil? There are people
who would never raise the cry 'Political Dissenters' if these latter
would quietly and unenquiringly pay rates and taxes, if they would
only be so far practically political as to further, like 'dumb, driven
cattle,' the designs of their 'superiors'. The moment however they
assume the quality of men, and take up the position in the state which as
men they should occupy, a chorus of denunciations, nicknames,
whinings and cries of alarm arises, the meaning of which is—'these
horrid *political* Dissenters are going to ruin the country'.

'Dissent is losing its influence as a Spiritual Body.' . . . On whom,
let us ask, is Dissent losing its influence as a spiritual body? Certainly
it is not losing power over members of the Church of England. Dissenters never exercised anything like the amount of that influence
which springs from holy living, over the clegy and pious laymen of
the Established Church which they do now. The proof may be found

in the innumerable instances of Christian intercourse and of fraternal cooperation, in works of Christian benevolence and of general service to the world.

Is it true then that Dissent is losing its influence as a spiritual body over the government of our country? No one acquainted with the history of his country during the last fifty years, unless led away by uncontrollable feelings or prejudice, would hazard such an assertion. Have we, as the Dissenting Churches, lost our spiritual power over the people? Every day's observation contradicts the truth of such an opinion. One of the chief indications of the influence possessed by one person or body of people over others is, that the influenced reposes confidence in the influencing party. Look at Dissenters in relation to the millions of their fellow countrymen. In the circumstances which outwardly belong to Dissenters, as a religious body, there is little to invite public attention. Nobles, esquires, magistrates, monied ladies and their patronage, gifts at certain seasons of the year of the liveries of charity, handsome windows, music and other apparent advantages, are either totally wanting, or are possessed only in a comparatively small degree by us. We do not say we should like all these auxiliaries as aids to distinction, influence and usefulness, but simply note that, whether we desiderate them or not, we cannot enumerate them among our attractions. Yet the people believe in, and trust, and look up to Dissenters for teaching and sympathy. We find according to Mr Mann's returns, that at the most numerously attended service on Census Sunday 1851, the attendance at Dissenting places of worship exceeded the attendance at the episcopal churches by nearly half a million people. 'But', it will be said, 'that fact does not prove that you are not a waning influence'. True, but this does—In 1801—assuming for the present that Dissenters were represented by the accommodation provided for purposes of worship among them—we had sittings for 963,169 persons. In 1851 we could accommodate 3,890,482; our increase in numbers, supposing sittings to represent our numbers, being at the rate of 407%!

Do these figures mean nothing in respect of spiritual influence? Look also at the constant increase of Sunday Schools. . . . Look also at the remarkable and gratifying increase of attendance at Dissenting chapels, particularly in large towns and cities. Consider too the readiness with which thousands of the people now listen to the gospel, who a few years since never entered church or chapel, and who, as abundantly proved in the rough experiences of that noble and indefatigable sect, the Primitive Methodists, were ready to annoy and to insult those who endeavoured to carry the truth of Christ within their hearing. At present, the highway is as safe as a spired edifice in those localities, while tens of thousands flock to halls, barns, warehouses, play-houses, as well as to chapels, to hear the way of salvation taught from Dissenting lips. It really seems marvellous that the good bishop should have selected this most favourable time in the history of Dissent as to spiritual power, in relation to the people, in order to bring forward his unjustifiable charge.

> Thomas Lloyd, *A Vindication of Dissent From the Misstatements Recently Made By the Lord Bishop of Gloucester and Bristol* (Ebley, 1860)

C Individualism

(i) *A religious view of laissez-faire*

We take government to be an organ for the protection of life, liberty and property; or, in other words, for the administration of justice. . . . We would dispatch it on no mission of knight-errantry in search of social felicity; it is much better kept at home to perform a less exalted task, but a task for which it is more fully qualified: let it leave its subjects, each for himself, in quiet pursuit of the greatest happiness, taking care only that none in his search trespass upon his neighbour's rights, or poach upon his neighbour's manor. Let it perform efficiently the duty of a police establishment and interfere with no man further than the demands of justice require, and it will then answer the end for which it is set up. If happiness be not the result, the fault is not in government— for the production of happiness lies not within its sphere.

> E. Miall, *The Nonconformist*, 1843, 633

(ii) *The basis of responsibility*

We see whole kingdoms . . . start from their slumber, the dignity of man rising up from depression, and tyrants trembling on their throne. . . . We need not wonder, if, amidst events so extraordinary the human character itself should appear to be altering and improving apace. . . . Man seems be to becoming more erect and independent. He leans more on himself, less on his fellow creatures. He begins to feel a consciousness in a higher degree of personal dignity, and is less enamoured of artificial distinctions. There is some hope of our beholding that simplicity

and energy of character which marks his natural state, blended with the
humanity, the elegance and improvement of polished society.

> O. Gregory (ed.), *The Works of the Rev.*
> *Robert Hall*, Vol. III (1831), 57 f.

D Democracy and political Dissent

As a result of events between 1832 and 1844, by debates and divisions
in Parliament; by organizations without, acting in concert; by kindred
agitations in the country; by the concordant testimony of its press—
the *Eclectic Review*, and the *Patriot*, and the *Nonconformist* newspapers—
by a participation in the same dark, ulterior counsels; by harbouring
the same suspicious and mutual sympathies, by a common hostility to
the British Constitution, though at first with somewhat different and
distinct fields of action—the Democrats assailing the civil, the Dissenters attacking the ecclesiastical institutions—lastly, by a communion of
struggles and risks encountered, Dissent became identified with, if not
allied to, Democracy; and the British Anti-State Church Association,
in 1844, established that alliance, if it were not contracted before. . . .
Toleration was admitted to be complete, but Dissent began to insist
upon the perfect equality of all religious sects; so, at the close of 1843,
we find Dissenters asserting a new claim to the perfect equality of all
mankind, in civil rights. Thus wrote the *Nonconformist* in its first
number for 1844: 'These two truths—the equal rights of man in political affairs, and the exclusive responsibility of man to God in spiritual
affairs—will be the pole star by whose clear light we shall pursue our
career'. . . .

Such were the first lessons of that new creed inculcated by the
Nonconformist. And, as with every other new prophet, Mr Miall's
first efforts were devoted to the instruction of his disciples. Accordingly
he started out with certain tangible, dogmatic principles, the basis of
which was Democracy in Church and State. . . .

Dissent by its ablest exponents is always associated with Democratic
institutions—with universal suffrage, the ballot, electoral districts,
annual parliaments and the payment of delegates. How then are such
institutions to consort with an hereditary aristocracy and an hereditary
monarchy? Democracy, aristocracy and monarchy require mutual
checks to coexist. But what check can there be upon an absolute
democracy, when the democratic element is actually in the high ascend-
ant and supreme? A perfect equality would be superinduced. The

majority of the people would allow of no equal, much less of any superior. Aristocracy and monarchy therefore would be extinguished by the same fiat which established those democratic institutions.

Now it is the boast of Dissent, that its very nature and essence are democratic. Once upon a time the *Electic Review* devoted an article to prove the contrary, but *tempora mutantur*. The *Liberator* now rejoices in appropriating what the *Electic* formerly repudiated as a reproach. With such a system then, as this, in active play, with free scope given to what is radically and fundamentally democratic, what room can there be either for the aristocratic or the monarchical principle to operate? Reverting indeed to what has been done, many achievements in the scene of action to which I now allude, have to be put down to the credit of political Dissent. Since 1844 uniformly, and since 1832 all but uniformly, Dissent has done its part in aiding and abetting all democratic inroads upon our civil institutions. During the years 1833 and 1837, two brief intervals, I grant that Dissent affected allegiance to the Whigs, but even that semblance soon disappeared. . . . Much, and indeed most, of that evanescent success attending the Ballot and Reform agitations, and whatever passes under that name, is to be attributed to the Anti-State Church party. As I have already shown, it was to the *Nonconformist* that the Complete Suffrage Union traced its origin. The same paper and its party stood sponsors for Chartism, and they formed the main strength and flower of the National Reform Association.

R. Masheder, *Dissent and Democracy* (1864),
96–8, 104–8, 393–6

E Social Science

A school of thinkers has of late arisen in England who make it their object to give to the term Sociology an exact scientific meaning. They start from the conception that human society, however complex its phenomena, however multiform its forces, is nevertheless a realm of law, in which nothing happens that could not, were our knowledge sufficiently minute and accurate, be traced to fixed and calculable causes. But for this fundamental thought, there could be no such thing as social science; for science involves prediction, and prediction is impossible if we admit any deviation from the straight line of causation. I will not presume to remark upon what is involved in this view of human action, or the important moral consequences to which it seems to lead; those who adopt it have the courage of their opinions, and address themselves in all good earnest to the apparently endless task of cataloguing phenomena, and bringing together likeness and unlikeness, and deducing laws:—all intended to lead up to some grand generalization of the final law of human development. But what I want you to observe is that social science so conceived is altogether an abstract, an intellectual thing. It watches society with the curious eye of the experimentalist, but it does not seek to raise, to strengthen, to purify it. . . . I can not, I am sure, be wrong in looking upon such a congress as that now assembled in Liverpool, as a meeting not of subtle-witted speculators, but of earnest moral reformers, each perhaps with his own special end in view, each with a somewhat differing conception of aim and method, but all profoundly convinced that social life is still infinitely remote from an ideal state, yet capable of being brought nearer to it by honest work and lavish self-denial. . . . The true strength of a united effort like this will, in any view, be found in proportion, as it is discerned to be a conscious striving after a Divine order of society. . . . The perfect society lies hidden beneath the grossness and deformity of our common life, like the statue to which the sculptor's skill will give everything but breath and motion in the whole block, rough-hewn from its quarrybed. But we shall never make it real till we reorganize it, not as our own commonwealth, but as the kingdom of God.

I wish with all my heart that I could honestly say that the teaching of the Christian Church as to the kingdom of God had always been clear and unvarying. Perhaps, if it had been, the work of Social Science Congresses, would not now remain to be done. Nothing can be to me more obvious than that in the mind of Christ the social work of Christianity was inseparable from its individual work; that its object was not merely the regenerate and transfigured man, but the regenerate and transfigured state. . . . In two ways, I am unwilling and ashamed to confess, the Church has been unfaithful to the profound conception and fine purpose of its Founder: it has thrown in its lot with the powers that be, preferring what it has called social order to social progress, and branding as infinitely dangerous all efforts from below to procure a reorganization of society: and again it has transformed the focus of religious interest from this world to another; has assumed that the kingdom of God can never be realized except in heaven, and has made even its heaven, long waited for in the ecstatic hope that kills present efforts, the happy legacy of the few, rather than the impartial inheritance of all. I need not further insist upon these things, with which you at least are sufficiently familiar: it is enough to record in the clearest and strongest terms which I am able to use, my conviction that neither will social strivings reach their desired goal, nor Christianity take its due place in the hearts of men, until all felt or unfelt antagonism between them is entirely removed.

Charles Beard, *The Kingdom of God, a Sermon preached to the 20th Annual Congress of the National Association for the Promotion of Social Science* (1876), 3–8

F Temperance

(i) *Pre-temperance days*

I have on a former occasion mentioned Stoney St Chapel. I ought to have said then that when the Queen was crowned (on June 28th, 1839) the Baptists were not behind any others in their manifestations of loyalty. A grand dinner was given to the Scholars. Two teachers besides myself fixed the tables in the grave yard, by driving short posts into the ground over the graves over which we placed the boards. We had a liberal supply of beef and plumb [*sic*] pudding, and I am sorry to say a quantity of Ale was likewise supplied to the children. The consequence was they became very demonstrative and we could not keep them in order as part of them were intoxicated. It was a sad sight to see such scenes with children of tender years feasting and drinking over the bodies of the dead along with those who ought to have known better.

J. Hopkinson, *Victorian Cabinet Maker*, ed.
J. B. Goodman (1968), 70–71

(ii) *Catechismal instruction*

Q 32. In what way does the use of intoxicating drinks affect the circumstances and comfort of those who take them?

A 1. By drinking habits a person loses the inclination as well as the ability to attend to his business; his business consequently declines, and this increases his propensity for intoxicating liquors, till ruin is the result.

2. On the other hand, by abstinence from all intoxicating liquors, money and time are saved, business is never neglected, and prosperity and comfort, personal and domestic, are secured.

3. Many delightful instances are continually occurring of the rapid and extraordinary improvement in the circumstances and happiness of those who have abandoned the use of intoxicating drinks. By habits of

excess they had reduced themselves and their families to poverty and
woe. Their prospects were blighted, their credit destroyed, and their
characters lost! But, by the blessing of God in the principles of total
abstinence from these liquors, they have again surrounded themselves
with comfort, regained their characters and credit, and become, in
many instances, sincere Christians.

Q 33. What will be the consequences of a habit of intemperance as
it regards a future state of existence?

A. It is impossible to contemplate the character and conduct of a
drunkard, without being convinced that such a person is altogether
unfit for the society of the blessed in heaven; and the Scriptures are
very explicit upon the subject—'Nor thieves, nor covetous, nor
drunkards etc. shall inherit the Kingdom of God'—1 Cor. vi. 10. . . .

Q 49. Are there any well-attested proofs that persons engaged in
laborious occupations do not need these stimulants?

A. Yes. In the registers of the society are the names and residences of
persons in all kinds of laborious employments; such as labourers in
town and country, carpenters, mechanics, manufacturers, smiths,
sawyers, smelters of ore, soldiers etc. etc. who can, and do, work harder
and longer, and with less fatigue upon good substantial food without a
drop of intoxicating liquor, than those who esteem it essentially necessary to their efforts. To these may be added seamen, who in all climates,
at all seasons of the year, in storms as well as in calms, have found
intoxicating liquors unnecessary. . . .

For a list of some few persons in these various classes, see Testimonies
published by Pasco, 90, Bartholomew Close, London: *To the Ladies of
England: Testimony of London Smiths and Cutlers: Testimonies of
Agricultural Labourers: The Danger of the Popular Use of Strong Drink
Medicinally: A Dry job, Master! May I beg a Drop of Gin?: The Convict:
The Working Man: You have been in the dram shop: You have been in
the jerry shop: I found you drunk: Dear Father, listen: Testimonies of
twelve sawyers: Is not a pint of ale good for a working man?: The Beacon
at sea, and gin lights on the land: The plague.*

A Manual of the new British and Foreign Temperance Society (1838), 11, 19

(iii) *An economic argument*

I come now to propose a most interesting and important measure;
The Total Abolition of the Poor Rates.

Is this a matter of no concern to the farmer, and the mechanic?

Not one of them but knows better than to say so. Is it enquired, would you be so cruel as to afford the poor no relief, no maintenance? I reply, Surely not, but I would put them in a way of making comfortable provision for themselves. There is money enough passes through the hands of our labouring population, to secure a share for old age and infirmities. The joint operation of the Savings Bank and Friendly Societies will avail for this laudable purpose. The poor rates are £8,000,000 a year, the prime cost of intoxicating drinks and tobacco is £56,000,000 a year: only one *seventh* then is required to be directed into a different channel to secure our object.

Let a labouring man enter a Friendly Society, and acting upon the tee-total principle, lay by £30 in the Savings Bank, the interest of this sum will pay his contributions to the club in case of sickness, and secure for him 9s. or 10s. a week. Is this a mere waking dream? By no means. Let farmers and manufacturers encourage their labourers and workmen to adopt this plan, let them reward them with money where they have given drink (especially in harvest) and the habits of sobriety learnt, and the increased wages received, will in not many years accomplish the desired end.

Let our agriculturalists and mechanics view it in what light they will, total abstinence from malting, brewing and distilling is their royal road to temporal (if not spiritual) prosperity. Let us be Tee-totallers, and have no more great Union-Houses. Let our poor be fed with barley, for it is now remarkable that the contracts entered into by the guardians on their behalf are for (gr)oats and oatmel. Let us see about turning our gaols and asylums into school houses and institutes, and so abolish another grievous burden, the County Rates. This too may be done by Tee-totalism; only cure the madness, and prevent the crime that proceeds from drinking instead of eating the barley, and the demand of the Quarter Sessions will rapidly decrease. We are all members one of another.

> So cry aloud, and never rest.
> For all, for all, Tee-Total's best.

H. Mudge, Surgeon, *Advice to Farmers and Other Employers with Testimonials In Favour of Tee-totalism*. Falmouth, The Cornwall Tee-total Tract Depository (n.d., c. 1840), 15–16

(iv)   *The difficulties in legislative solutions*

The production of this Permissive Bill, and the conducting of the agitation in its favour, have been the sole work of the United Kingdom
Alliance for twenty years. It has conducted its agitation with great
vigour. It has been well served by its officers and lecturers and parliamentary agents. The expenditure of money has been lavish. The means
adopted, especially in regard to parliamentary elections have been at
times unscrupulous and fanatical in a wonderful degree. The result of
the Alliance agitation thus far has been, we fear, to prevent the passing
of useful practical measures, and to hinder the action of the healthy
educational influence which the older temperance movement originated. . . .

Our objections to the Permissive Bill touch it at many points. As
a remedy for our national vice, it does not deal with the man who has
contracted the vicious habit, but with the outward circumstances
in which he has found opportunity for his wicked indulgences. It
relies neither on teaching, sympathy nor example, for restoring the
intemperate, but on force. It does not aim at making the man stronger,
but cuts off the temptation which acts upon his weakness. That the
removal of temptation may play an important part in this, as in other
works of moral reform, we heartily admit; but it can never be the
leading, much less the sole, expedient of the reformer, if his work is not
to be a mere cleansing of the outside of the cup and platter. . . .

Our main hope is in moral influence. A great free people will not
ultimately give up even a vice which is eating its vitals because of
material obstacles placed in the way of its indulgence. What it will yield,
it may be by a slow process, to the teaching of science, the example
and sympathetic counsel of good men, and the higher influences of
religion, it will deny to the imperious demand of law. And nothing
could be more fatal to true progress in all that concerns our national
sobriety, than the prevalence of the belief that the virtuous and religious part of the community can discharge its obligations concerning
intemperance by promoting legislative measures for its suppression. On
no such easy terms can we become the helpers of our tempted and fallen
brethren, and so the saviours of the society which their vicious ways are
bringing into peril. The rich and well-to-do must live more among the
poor. They must set them an example of self-control, of freedom from
luxury, and superiority to the temptations of their own station. They
must aid them in their struggle with the disadvantages of their lot.
If this seems to postpone the millennium of temperance reformers for

an indefinite period, we may comfort ourselves with the belief that
that millennium when it comes will be an assured and permanent
triumph.

British Quarterly Review, Volume 64 (1876),
116–18, 128–9

(v)   *A social crusade*

1

Amid the splendour of the spring
The glory of its flowers,
The joyous songs the wild birds sing,
One constant grief is ours:
Grief for the homes no spring can reach,
Hearts that no sun can cheer,
Souls that no happy warblings teach
The lesson of the year.

2

Where gloomy alleys thickly crowd,
The children, pinched and pale,
Hear angry voices harsh and loud,
Hear suffering's bitter wail;
While the sweet daisied meads of God,
Clad in his gift of green,
Call to the feet that have not trod,
Eyes that no fields have seen.

3

Oh dark upon the children falls
The shadow of the strife
That robs them of their festivals
And holy days of life;
Drink is that shadow stern and grim;
Christians! Awake and pray;
Cry to your Lord for grace from Him
This curse to drive away.

4

He loves the children, who hath given
His life to save and heal;
His spring-time symbols hope and heaven
And doth His life reveal.

Oh! for new growth of faith and prayer,
Work that a world shall free,
Out of the shadow and despair
To pass to victory.

The Primitive Methodist Hymnal, Supplement
no. 236

G   The Friendly Society

As long ago as 1818, the evil effect of public house Friendly
Societies occupied the attention of our Church officers; and in consequence of a direct application from some members, who were
labourers and artizans, a code of rules was drawn up, and the deacons
conceded to them the occasional use of a schoolroom for their meetings,
and a supply of candles when necessary. The club was then formed. It
chose its treasurer, and subsequently, when the funds had increased,
trustees, in whose names the surplus money is from time to time
invested. It has never been of any expense to the Dissenting interest
than what is mentioned above. The club speedily grew in numbers,
and by a steady progression has accumulated a fair amount of property.
It is of course open to persons of any religious opinion, and contains
many of every persuasion in our neighbourhood.

There have been admitted since its formation in 1818 . . . 457
members. It has lost by death 164. There are at this time 293. Its receipts
from members' subscriptions and interest in capital amount to £4,442.
It has paid for sickness, deaths etc. £3,854. Its present capital is £588.

Of this sum £517 is at interest on mortgage securities; a part of the
remainder bears interest from the treasurer, and is waiting for a little
increase to be also put out; and the rest is floating capital with the
stewards. Each member subscribes one shilling per month to the general
fund, sixpence per quarter for medical attendance, and one shilling on
the death of every member who has belonged to the club for twelve
months, or sixpence if he has joined it within that period. The payments
are eight shillings per week, for any duration of sickness, not less than
a week, nor more than twelve months, and sixpence for any time beyond
this. Three shillings per head for the total number of members is
paid to the medical attendant; and the whole of the money, gathered
for each death, to the family of the deceased.

We should have probably been much stronger both in men and
money, but for the formation of another club in a neighbouring village,

formed after our model, and meeting in the schoolroom of a Dissenting church, which our good minister had the honour of planting there. The comparative youthfulness of its members has attracted the young towards it, somewhat to our loss. Having fewer demands on their stock, they have acquired property more rapidly, and are much richer in proportion than we. They have 220 members and a capital of £750.

We have also a women's club, which has been established about twenty two years, for affording aid in sickness and confinement. It has now about a hundred members and a capital of about £100. You will notice it is much poorer than the other two; proceeding from the more frequent sickness of females, the greater inducement to imposture, and the greater difficulty of detecting it.

The Christian Witness, Volume 2 (1845), 224

H   The Sunday School

(i)   *Potentials and difficulties*

We have thought that, without committing ourselves to any undue eulogy on the subject, it may not be amiss to call the attention of our readers to some of the more obvious of the benefits attendant upon this effort to advance popular education, and to secure to it the best direction by allying it more effectually than is practicable in day-schools with moral and religious principles. These benefits have respect to three classes—the teachers, the children, and the community.

I. The *teachers* of every Sunday School may be described as a voluntary corporation, forming its own laws, and self-regulated in all its proceedings. . . . The fraternity of the Sunday-school is to the teacher as a little commonwealth, in which all those principles and feelings are to be first brought into play which are to fit him for the discharge of his duty in the greater commonwealth of the church or the world. . . . The influence of the office of Sunday School teacher on self-cultivation in general is too obvious to be overlooked. The man who would teach must learn. . . . In cheap publications which appear from month to month facilities are presented. . . . That the teachers may be qualified, the Suday School has its library, consisting generally of a collection of books well suited to their purpose. . . . Then, in most instances, teachers have their periodical meetings for mutual instruction. . . . Such is this great educational class of the community. It consists of young persons who, in this manner, are made to be familiar with the more useful forms of public business; with the principles of order necessary to every self-governed body; and with the method by which many things may be done, and each at its best time and in its best manner. ... In this Great School there is always at least a quarter of a million of our Youth passing through these processes of self-education. Truly we should have a sorry opinion of the educationalist or statesman who should ever seem to account this fact as other than deeply interesting and momentous. ... No other nation has ever seen the same extent of self-sustained, self-organized and self-regulated intelligence and piety, in the same class of persons.

II. The class whose benefit is ostensibly sought in these institutions consists of *children*. ... With the children of the operative and labouring classes, attendance at day school ceases early, very many of them being sent to some kind of employment before they are twelve years of age. It is when attendance at the day-school ceases that Sunday-school instruction becomes especially valuable. Great numbers who would otherwise have forgotten the little they had learned, are thus retained in some habit of reading, and are thus encouraged, in their effort to add to their little stock of knowledge. ...

But it is in the moral and religious character of the instruction given in Sunday-school that its chief distinction and value consist. We have before said, and we repeat, we have no great opinion of the religious knowledge which can be or is communicated in a common day school. ... If the Sunday-school does not intervene to correct the children of the common day school with a religious influence, they commonly drift off into the world, and become wholly lost to such influence. So important is the mission of our Sunday-schools in respect to that large portion of the community, the children of our operative and labouring classes—those who are to become the fathers and mothers of three quarters of the next generation!

But there are two great defects in this otherwise valuable system of appliances. It does not retain its hold long enough on the older scholars; and it does not expand and adapt itself so as to take in classes of children who are not sufficiently clean, or accustomed to mix with children of a somewhat better class than themselves, to be in place in our ordinary Sunday-school.

With regard to the first defect, some spirited attempts have been made to remove it by the formation of Bible-classes. ... While this improvement is needed at one end of the system, there is another no less needed at the other end. Those children of the lowest class, of which we have spoken—those ragged outcasts from all culture and decency—if they are ever to be reached, it must be, we conceive, by an extension of the branch Sunday-school plan. . . . Why should not every great city and every considerable town possess its branch school association, consisting of benevolent and pious persons of all religious connections, who should direct their labours to the lowest section of the population?

III. The effect of Sunday schools in relation to the *community* it is not easy to estimate. We know enough to be assured that it must be manifold and vast; *but*, the real extent of this influence can only be a matter of conjecture. . . . We are warranted in concluding that the Sunday-schools connected with the different bodies of Nonconformists in our towns and great cities and through our manufacturing districts, are considerably more than double the number connected with the Church of England. We must venture to say also that, making allowances for instances of exception, the schools connected with the Nonconformists are much more efficient than those connected with the state church. This arises in part from the difference between the Conformist and Nonconformist systems. The tendencies of the latter are more favourable to self-reliance and independent action; and the teachers are not only more zealous and competent, but exist in much greater proportion as compared with the number of scholars. In the support of common day schools however Churchmen are greatly in advance of Nonconformists; partly from their greater wealth, and the greater leisure of their clergy, and partly from their preponderating influence through the rural districts.

> *British Quarterly Review*, Volume 1 (1845), 54 f.

(ii) *A call to Christian parents*

The Sunday School is at present only a missionary enterprise. It ought to be used for the good of those in the congregation as well as those out of it. Christian parents and educated Christian parents should send their children to Sunday School, so that rich and poor may be taught together. We cannot too earnestly protest against the invidious class distinction which at present exists between the children of the Sunday School and those of the congregation. There ought to be no such distinction as far as religious teaching is concerned. The preacher addresses both classes in his congregation—rich and poor—and is understood, and his teaching is appreciated by both. Why should it not be so also with the Sunday School teacher? The fears entertained by parents as to the injurious effects of such a mingling of the classes are very groundless. There would be no more intercourse between the scholars than would be for the good of all, while the young of the congregation would receive such a teaching as would influence them in all future days.

S. Pearson, *The Evangelical Magazine*, Volume 10 (New Series, 1868), 30

I   A Nonconformist view of trade unions

. . . the movement which commenced a few months since in Warwickshire, and which is spreading gradually over the whole agricultural region of south and mid-England, is not unlike the first of those upheavals which occurred five centuries ago. Like that, it is an attempt to escape from what was felt to be an intolerable and hopeless bondage, with the difference that, on the former occasion, the insurrectionists aimed at a relief from arbitrary service, while the present is an attempt, through the machinery of a similar combination, to exact better terms for manual labour. Just as the poor priests of Wickliffe's training were the agents, perhaps unintentionally, by whom communications were made between the various disaffected regions, so on the present occasion the ministers or preachers of those humbler sects, whose religious impulses are energetic, and perhaps sensational, have been found the national leaders of a struggle after social emancipation. A religious revival has constantly been accompanied by an attempt to better the material condition of those who are the objects of the impulse. It may be doubted, indeed, whether any movement in a religious direction has ever been successful unless it has been coupled with a determination to improve the social and moral condition of those who join it, or at least has invited its disciples or converts to discover a compensation for the hardships and wrongs of life in the consolations of religion, or in the hopes of some judicial restitution. In the earlier attempts to obtain a change, the spirit of the time led to the use of violent means towards the end, and this spirit continued up to comparatively recent times. A generation ago the agricultural labourer strove to arrest the operation of changes which seemed adverse to him, and of laws which oppressed him, by machine breaking and rick burning. These efforts were, to be sure, insulated and spasmodic, and of course failed of making any impression on the facts which they were intended to controvert. Now the agricultural labourer has adopted the machinery of a trade union and a strike, and has conducted his agitation in a strictly peaceful and law-abiding manner.

A trade union, with its occasional and permanent concomitants, is by no means the best form by which social inequalities and unfairness may be remedied; but it is, under existing circumstances, nearly the only means towards this end. . . . It has been doubted, and perhaps with some justice, whether in England, at least, these associations have had the effect of raising wages. It is contended, and with great appearance of truth, that workmen have been in the various mechanical trades so much in demand, that the principle of competition for the employment of labour has had full play, and that the rise of wages among artisans and factory operatives is to be ascribed to natural, and not to artificial causes. But it cannot be doubted that workmen's associations have shortened the hours of labour, have educated artisans—as they will the agricultural labourer—into the sense of a common interest and a common duty, and have made the interests of the working classes so notable a matter of public interest, that political parties are fain to attempt association with them, and to legislate for them. The demands of the artisans in the Midland and Northern counties exacted the factory acts (laws, by the way, which were passed against the opposition of the Conservative party, and not, as the expositors of this party are fond of saying, at their instance and by their assistance), the workmen having discovered by rule of thumb that long working hours are not cheap labour, a position long since demonstrated by Mr. Edwin Chadwick, and abundantly confirmed by facts. At the same time it must be admitted, in justice to those employers of labour who opposed the acts in question, that they believed great national interests to be imperilled by the legislation; and it is also true that the country party, which is fond of asserting that it assisted in their passage, has strenuously resisted the extension of the acts to agricultural districts

The low wages of agricultural labourers are really assisted by the poor rate. In some parts of England the habit of giving out-door relief to the able-bodied but destitute poor has grown into a practice which is reproducing some of the features of the old allowance system. Of course such a state of things can arise only when the wages of labour are so low, that the recipient is, even when in full work, on the very verge of destitution, and when, therefore, a temporary cessation from his customary employment leaves him nothing with which to provide for the necessities of his family. In those cases where a rural district is added to a thriving town, or the suburb of a thriving town, the temptation on the part of the farmer guardians to give this form of out-door relief in aid of wages is almost irresistible, since, by adopting the expedient, they find themselves able to lighten the cost of the labour from which they get their profit, at the charge of those, who being ratepayers, do not employ labour with any such view of profit, and therefore do not directly contribute to the pauperism of the district. But in so far as the tenant farmer pays rates, his outgoings are increased and his profits diminished. Now, although it is out of the question that agricultural labourers receiving some ten to twelve shillings a week in the average of the year, can find the means for their own maintenance in sickness and old age; as they can hardly be expected to belong to a provident society, or even to meet any of the least risks wich attend their calling, by economy and saving, yet it is very conceivable that when the wages of labourers are raised, and they receive a more plentiful reward for their services, they will be able to meet these contingencies, and exercise that thrift and forethought, the absence of which people are very often induced to deplore, without asking themselves whether they have any right, even from the most sanguine point of view, to expect them under existing circumstances. . . .

It cannot be too often insisted on, or too thoroughly remembered, that the progress of public opulence does not consist so much in the fact that wealth is accumulated, but in the evidence that it is generally distributed, that it is no great matter of interest to know the process by which a few get rich, as it is to discover the means by which the many can be contented and comfortable; and that it is idle to expect that society will ever be free from those fears which alarm, and the facts which occasionally disturb it, as long as men can point to the extreme poverty of the many, and the unbounded opulence of the few. This, at least, is clear. The prosperity of trade is closely connected with the distribution of wealth, and society, as a body of producers and consumers, need show little respect for its accumulation.

With greater comfort and contentment come more independence, more enterprise, and a higher standard of decency, morality, and religion. It is an error to imagine that independence makes men unmanageable or unreasonable. Few men take a more intelligent estimate of their position than English artisans do. When they do unite for co-operative purposes they show no symptom of insubordination or disobedience to the necessary orders of their managers or directors. The success with which co-operation and co-operative banking have been introduced into Northern Germany is evidence of the readiness with which working men can associate for the purpose of bettering themselves in accordance with intelligible and sound social principles, and how they are able to repudiate that plausible but mischievous sophistry which, under one or another form of Communism, holds out such golden visions to the imagination of those who think that they can reconstruct society. But assuredly there is no reason to think that the English agricultural labourer can sink to any lower level than that which he occupies now. It is notorious that poverty constrains him to set aside the decencies of life, that a peasant's cottage is a hotbed of corruption, and that a glance at a criminal calendar in the agricultural districts is conclusive evidence as to the vices of our English Arcadia. Under such influences, it is no wonder that the religious sense of the peasantry is obtuse; the marvel is that it should exist at all, and be capable of being stirred by the homely but earnest eloquence of the Methodist preacher, the apostle of the agricultural labourer. In the last session of Parliament Sir Roundell Palmer, taking up the defence of the Anglican Establishment, against the motion of Mr Miall, invited the attention of the House to the beneficent functions which are performed by the country clergy. If, indeed, they are to be responsible for the condition in which their flocks are found, no severer censure of their efforts can be uttered than Sir Roundell Palmer's praise; for it is not too much to say that nine-tenths of the religion which the agricultural labourer believes is gained in spite of the clergy, and by agencies which they name only to scorn or ridicule.

'The Agricultural Labourers' Strike', *British Quarterly Review*, July 1872, 157–68

J The Poor

(i) *'Abject and lost lay these'*

In all communities and especially in large cities and towns, there are sinks of iniquity into which all the sores and all the filth of society naturally run and empty themselves—where squalid poverty, heathenish ignorance and brutal sensuality are found in dreadful combination. Here vice runs for indulgence—crime for shelter—vagrancy for a halting place—and shame, ruin and misfortune to hide their heads. Sometimes these places are found in contiguity with wealth, rapid improvement, and even with the highest religious advantages. . . . I have seen a little—a very little—of such places. I have sometimes (though too seldom) ventured with tracts from house to house, and from chamber to chamber, talking to the wretched inmates. The impression generally left on my mind was that the poor creatures seemed to live in a world of their own, where their minds were as much cooped in as their bodies, and where they naturally grovelled

and weltered, never venturing to lift their heads so far as to look on
society above them or to be conscious that there were such things as
comfort, cleanliness, reputation, knowledge, or religion in the world.

> —'So thick bestrewn,
> Abject and lost lay these.'

I have felt that if there were a church, a chapel, and a school at the
entrance of every alley, the forlorn and sunk inhabitants would never
look at any of them—perhaps hardly know of their existence.

On such places as these I have two remarks to make; first, that they
must almost be left out of the account in any estimate of the sufficiency
of the means of education, because the classes herding there would not,
and in their present state could not, make any use of such provision, be
it as abundant as it might; and second, that these places, whilst they
challenge the pity and courage of Christian zeal to undertake the Her-
culean labour of cleansing them, are out of the reach of government
interference, except in the way of a restraining police. There is no power
in Government to raise these abjects, to shed the ray of hope in their
minds, to kindle the extinct feelings of love and gratitude in their
bosoms, to bring penitence to such hardened hearts, to awaken in them
an idea of God and eternity. It is to your Howards, your Frys, your
Nasmiths—to men and women filled with concern for perishing
souls—to ministers of Religion and Town missionaries—to Tract
distributors, Bible readers, agents of Female Guardian Societies, and
Sunday School Teachers—that such enterprises must be left. And
after all, do what they will, it is to be feared that these sinks will never
be emptied, because every day is refilling them.

E. Baines Junior, *Letters to Lord John Russell on
State Education* (1846), 22–3

(ii) *The churches' contribution and neglect*

The claims of God by his Son, our Lord and Saviour, presented to men
through the medium of our religious organizations, although not
generally met, on the part of the humbler classes, with settled unbelief and bitter antipathy, fail to awaken interest, almost to excite
notice. The Principality of Wales stands out, it must be confessed, as a
cheering exception. The several sections of Methodism too in this
country have done enough to prove that the masses may be permeated
and subdued by divine truth when aptly and fervently enforced upon
them. Indeed but for their assiduous attention to the poor, their

comparative disregard of social distinctions in their ecclesiastical
economy, and their wise adaptation of means to ends in their machinery
of aggression upon the world, it is hard to conceive what would now
have been the desperate spiritual conditions of the working classes of
this country. Nor am I disposed to deny that the Churches of other
denominations attach to themselves, and operate upon, individuals
moving in the sphere of poverty, in varying proportions, But there are
few, I should imagine, who will controvert the statement that religious
profession, and respect for the public means of grace, are far more common amongst, and characteristic of, the middle, than the labouring
classes, in Great Britain. The bulk of our manufacturing population
stand aloof from our Christian institutions. An immense majority of
those who in childhood attend our Sabbath schools neglect throughout
the period of manhood, all our ordinary appliances of spiritual instruction and culture. When disease creeps upon them or death looks
them in the face, early association may have power enough over many
to induce them to send for a minister of the Gospel, and request his
conversation and his prayers. But evidence is abundant and conclusive
that they generally pass through the prime of life, and too frequently
reach its appointed term, without being even momentarily attracted,
and without being in the slightest degree interested, by what the
Churches of Christ are doing in their respective neighbourhoods. The
operatives of these realms, taken as a body, and the still more numerous
class whose employment is less regular, and whose temporal prospects
are still more discouraging and precarious, must be described as living
beyond even occasional contact with the institutions of Christian
faith and worship. . . . The Churches which, if they were true to the
spirit of their mission and the design of their Lord . . . might and
ought to have won from this over-burdened, underfed and sorely
neglected class, a general confidence, resembling that formerly given
by negro slaves to missionaries in the West Indies—the Churches
which should have turned the very hardships and privations and
unbefriended lowliness of these people, to account, by offering to
them the respect due to their nature and the commiseration due to
their conditions, and whenever it was possible countenance, counsel
and aid—the Churches are, to all practical purposes, as little known,
as little cared for, as little trusted in, by this numerous body, as if they
had no existence.

E. Miall, *The British Churches in Relations to
the British People* (1849), 221–4

(iii)   *The folly of snobbery*

There is growing up even in our Dissenting churches, an evil which I greatly deplore—a despising of the poor. I frequently hear, in conversation, such remarks as this: 'It is of no use trying in such a place as this: you could never raise a self-supporting cause. There are none but poor living in this neighbourhood.' . . . You know that in the city of London itself, there is now scarce a Dissenting place of worship. The reason for giving most of them up and moving them into the suburbs is that all the respectable people live out of town, and of course they are the people to look after. They will not stop in London. They will go out and take villas in the suburbs; and therefore the best thing is to take the endowment that belonged to the old chapel, and go and build a new chapel somewhere in the suburbs where it may be maintained. 'No doubt', it is said, 'the poor ought to be looked after: but we had better leave them to another order, an inferior order. The city missionaries will do for them; send them a few street preachers.'

C. H. Spurgeon from a sermon of 26 May
1861

(iv)   *A radical's sermon*

On Sunday morning in company with these Chartist friends I went and spoke in the open air at Fenton and in the afternoon at Longton. In the evening I addressed an immense crowd at Hanley, standing on a chair in front of the Crown Inn: such ground being called the Crown Bank by the natives. I took for a text the sixth commandment: 'Thou shalt do no murder'—after we had sung Bromwich's hymn 'Brittania's sons, though slaves ye be', and I had offered a short prayer.

I showed how kings in all ages had enslaved the people, and spilt their blood in wars of conquest, thus violating the precept, 'Thou shalt do no murder'.

I named conquerors from Sesostris to Alexander, from Caesar to Napoleon, who had become famous in history by shedding the blood of millions; thus violating the precept, 'Thou shalt do no murder'.

I recounted how English and French and Spanish and German wars in modern history had swollen the list of slaughtered and thus violated the precept, 'Thou shalt do no murder'.

I described how the conquerors of America had nearly exterminated the native races, and thus violated the precept, 'Thou shalt do no murder'.

I rehearsed the plunder of the Church by Henry VIII and the burning of men and women for religion by himself and his daughter Mary who thus violated the precept, 'Thou shalt do no murder'.

I described our own guilty colonial rule, and still guiltier rule in Ireland, and asserted that British rulers had most awfully violated the principle, 'Thou shalt do no murder'.

I showed how the immense taxation we were forced to endure to enable our rulers to maintain the long and ruinous war with France and Napoleon had entailed indescribable suffering on millions; and that thus had been violated the principle 'Thou shalt do no murder'.

I asserted that the imposition of the bread tax was a violation of the same precept, and that such was the enactment of the Game Laws; that such was the custom of primogeniture and keeping of the land in the possession of the privileged classes; and that such was the enactment of the infamous new Poor Law.

The general murmur of applause now began to swell into loud cries; and these were mingled with execrations of the authors of the Poor Law—I went on.

I showed that low wages for wretched agricultural labourers and the brutal ignorance in which generation after generation they were left by the landlords was a violation of the principle. 'Thou shalt do no murder'.

I asserted that the attempt to lessen the wages of toilers underground, who were in hourly and momentary danger of their lives and to disable them from getting the necessary food for themselves and their families, were violations of the precept 'Thou shalt do no murder'.

I declaimed that all who were instrumental in maintaining the system of labour which reduced poor stockingers to the starvation I had witnessed in Leicester—and which was witnessed among the poor handloom weavers of Lancashire and poor nailmakers of the Black Country—were violating the precept, 'Thou shalt do no murder'.

And now the multitude shouted; and their looks told of vengeance—but I went on, for I felt as if I could die on the spot in fulfilling a great duty—the exposure of human wrong and consequent human suffering. My strength was great at the time, and my voice could be heard like the peal of a trumpet, even to the verge of a crowd composed of thousands. How sincere I was, God knows, and it seemed impossible for me, with my belief of wrong to act otherwise.

I fear I spent so much time in describing this wrong, and raising the spirit of vengeance in those who heard me that the little time I spent in conclusion, and in showing that those who heard me were not to

violate the precept , 'Thou shalt do no murder', either literally or in its
spirit, but that they were to practise the Saviour's commandment, and
to forgive their enemies, produced little effect in the way of lowering
the flame of desire for vengeance, or raising the spirit of gentleness and
forgiveness.

> T. Cooper, *Life Written by Himself* (1877),
> 187–90

(v) *The submerged tenth*

The men who are trampling upon traditional customs, the women who
are publicly preaching, the bands and processions which are seeking to
awaken attention, represent a spirit which says to the churches and
regular ministries—'Here is a great work to be done, will you do it or
will you not? If you will not attempt it, then do not, in the name
of the living God who will have all men to be saved, hinder those
who are willing to assume the tremendous task; but, whilst you are
organising conferences, adjusting resolutions, heaping together funds
for bishoprics and palaces, the devil triumphs, men die, hell is moved
from beneath, and the Cross is branded as the failure of God! We are
unlearned and ignorant men, and have no wish to interfere with
trained ministers, regular channels and venerable traditions, but if
these men and methods fail, or slumber, or hesitate, we must undertake
the responsibility of doing what in our power lies to avert the doom
which is coming on our country, we must make our voices to be heard
amidst the blasphemy of the age, and if we are interfering with hoary
customs, vested interests, concealed idolatries or honest incapacity,
we will remit the controversy to the arbitrament of God.' Personally
I am prepared to recognize in that ardent challenge the sacred passion
of a heart that is at one with the purpose of the Cross.[1] . . . God is
love—What but love—love of God, love of Christ, love of man—
could live and work with anxious hopefulness, in some parts of the very
London in which we are now gathered? No words can fitly describe
the awful circumstances. We cannot indeed properly pronounce the
words which even dimly indicate the perdition, the smoke of whose
torment beclouds the splendour of our garish civilization. Only a
man who has known the pain of hunger can properly pronounce the
word 'hunger': it is part of a foreign language to us; we know its letters,
we do not know its gnawing cruelty, but he knows all the horrors of

[1] The description relates to the expanding work of the Salvation Army in
down-town areas.

the expressive term. Gentility turns aside from the darker features of the times: pedantry asks for rising neighbourhoods and social distinctions: self-indulgence is anxious about its smoking feast and downy couch: speculation prays that its serene retreat be unviolated by the noise of vulgar tragedies: vanity exhausts itself in petty idolatries: learning plans an extension of its library—still, the appalling facts remain, a daily appeal to Christian attention, still, the little child dies in the foetid room; the reeling drunkard staggers to his bed of straw; ruined womanhood cries for vengeance; pale hunger dies in silence; discontentment plots the downfall of society, bold blasphemy drowns the plea of timid prayer; still the darkness lengthens its deadly shadow, and still the pit widens into a gloomier abyss; and in the face of facts which are their own eloquence I venture to contend that the only force equal to the overwhelming occasion is a sanctified heart, a love like Christ's own, a compassion large and soft as the pity of God.

I have supposed a speech to be delivered to us by men who wish to take up Christian work whose only education is the inspiration of love. I can hear another speech still more poignant and impatient in tone. Imagine the gathered hordes of ignorance, misfortune, misery and shame, having gone the rounds of all the Unions, Conferences, Assemblies and Convocations, held in the course of the ecclesiastical year: imagine one of the members of that suffering community representing his comrades, and putting their sorrows and wishes into words, and his speech might take some such turn as this—'We have had a full year among you, and we cannot very well make out what you are driving at. We do not know most of the long words you use. You are all well-dressed and well-fed and you are D.D.'s and M.A.'s and B.A.'s We do not know what you are, or what you want to be at. From what we can make out you seem to know that we poor devils are all going straight down to a place you call hell: there we are to burn for ever and ever and gnash our teeth in pain that can never end: we are to be choked with brimstone, stung by serpents, laden with chains: then why don't you stop us on the road? Why don't you stand in front of us, and keep us back from the pit and the fire and the worm that cannot die? We read the inky papers which you call your "resolutions", but in them there is no word for us that is likely to do us real good. They say nothing about our real misery; nothing about our long hours, our poor pay, our wretched lodgings.' . . . If I might add a word on an immediately related question, it be to the effect that our evangelism is in danger of devoting itself almost exclusively to what are known as 'the masses'. I must protest against this contraction, on the ground that

it is as unjust to Christianity, as it is blind to the evidence of facts. If the
city missionary (he being a highly qualified man) is wanted anywhere,
he is specially wanted where business is degraded into gambling, where
conscience is lulled by charity which knows nothing of sacrifice, and
where political economy is made the scapegoat for oppression and
robbery. But to lecture the poor is easier than to accuse the rich. Have
we not lost one bold tone out of the music of preaching? Who now
dares say, 'Ye adulterers and adulteresses, know ye not that the friendship of the world is enmity with God? Whosoever therefore will be
a friend of the world is the enemy of God' (James 4, 4); 'Woe unto you
that are rich, for ye have received your consolation' (Luke 6, 24);
'Behold the hire of the labourers who have reaped down your fields,
which is of you kept back by fraud, crieth; and the cries of them which
have reaped are entered into the ears of the Lord of Sabaoth' (James 5,
4)? That is a branch of evangelistic service which cannot be neglected
with impunity. There is only one class worse than the class known as
'outcast London'—worse in every feature and in every degree—and
that class is composed of those who 'have lived in pleasure on the
earth and been wanton', and who have 'nourished their hearts as in
a day of slaughter'. The cry is 'bitterer'[2] in many tones at the West End
than at the East; the ennui, the lure of pleasure, the satiety of appetite,
the speculation in marriage, the gambling in politics, the thousand
social falsehoods that mimic the airs of Piety and claim the protection
of Usage—these seem to be distresses without alleviation, and to constitute a heathenism which Christ himself might view with despair.

> From the address of the Chairman, the
> Reverend Dr Joseph Parker, *The Congrega-
> tional Year Book* (1885) 59–63

(vi) *A judgement on hypocrisy*

DOWN WHITECHAPEL WAY.

'Certain manufacturing companies, whose shareholders receive 20 per cent.
on their capital therein, pay many of their employés at a rate by which they
can earn three farthings an hour, or about three shillings for six days of
twelve hours' labour.'

O DON'T I wish I was ill again, that I might go where the ladies sing,
And tell one about the lovely fields where they gather the nosegays they always
  bring:
For down in our court 'tisn't hymns we hear, save sometimes trolled as a drunken
  song;
And if some of us gets a bit put out, we pitches our language pretty strong!

[2] A reference to A. Mearns, *The Bitter Cry of Outcast London* (1883).

Why, father himself—but to speak the truth, and yet be fair to the poor old dad,
If he isn't so very, very drunk, he isn't so very, very bad.
Mother gets out of his way those nights, or he'd beat her till she was black and blue;
But she only says it is all because the London pubs sell such fiery brew.

An' she owns she's sharp o' the tongue and cross; but if she is, is she much to blame?
There's no fine clothes for her, as there is for the girls that she calls by the awful
    name:
And she's no nice room like our nurses had, with flowers and pictures and friends
    to call,
But a three-pair back where the washing swings and father must work and the
    babies squall.

I wonder sometimes how mother'd look in a clean white cap and a lilac gown?
Yet I'll never see her in such, I guess, though the parsons promise us robe and
    crown,
An' silver gateways and streets o' gold—and I hope the angels can keep them clean,
An' that folks won't crowd into heaven so thick as not to leave us a bit o' green!

But there's some don't believe what the parsons say—and one's the tailor who
    lives downstairs,
Who uses the Bible to light his pipe, and scoffs at prayer, though he always swears;
And there's Long Dick, too, of another sort, sober and decent and kind and fair,
Who thinks that the world could not be what it is, if there was a Father above to
    care.

And he's so sorry to fear there ain't, that he tries to care for the world himself;
I've known him give to a starving boy all the food he had on his little shelf—
(I was that boy, so I ought to know); and though he isn't the sort that fights,
Women and children—and cats and dogs—know to look to Dick when they want
    their rights!

Says I to Long Dick this day last week, 'I believe there's a God, because there's you!
Where do you come from, Dick,' says I, 'if the best that they tell of Him isn't true?'
But now Dick's going abroad, he says, to seek some place where the sunshine's
    free;
Perhaps he'll find God in the far, far West, and I trust God will still keep an eye on
    me!

I'd go myself, but I'm just too old to be taken out as the children are,
And the gentlemen folk that I've spoken to, say I'm not the sort that should travel
    far;
They pinch my muscles, and shake their heads. 'There's no farm-labour in him,'
    they say—
So there's nothing better in store for me than a coster's barrow Whitechapel way!

That's why I wish I was ill again, that I might go where the lady sings—
For there's one in special that always comes, and speaks so sweetly of holy things.
She's wife o' the head of the firm that owns the great match factory near our court—
But always when I begins on her, Long Dick turns grumpy and cuts me short.

Says he, 'There's no one knows more than me that we're bad and ugly and coarse
    and low,

But I'd rather be us,' says Dick, 'than the gents whose money-making has made us
    so;
And who live apart in their pleasant homes that have their root in our toil and pain,
And preach of Heaven and God to us whose blood is on all the gold they gain.

'Don't let none prate about "doing good" till they're trying their hardest to just
    do right;
If there is the God that they talk about, they're viler than we are in His sight,
With their twenty per cent. for doing naught, while our women slave for three
    bob a week—
Let them stop that short ere they take to preach, and I'll be the readiest to hear
    them speak.'

And there comes such a light in Long Dick's blue eyes—but then he was country-
    bred you see;
You can't expect that sort of a pluck in Londoner chaps brought up like me:
We're either ready to rob and rive, so we drink our liquor and dance our fling—
Or we weakly wish we were always ill, that we might stay where the ladies sing!
    Aberdeen, Aug. 8th.   ISABELLA FYVIE MAYO.
                        British Weekly, July 1887

K   Internationalism

War dislocates all industry; engulfs all savings; loads countries with
debt; lessens the comforts, the decencies, and even the necessaries of
every family; ravages wide districts; maims, mutilates or slays thousands and tens of thousands of the adult male population, the very
pick of the people, and in the prime of their youthful vigour; corrupts
the character and cripples the progress of the nations which engage in
it. The burden of all this falls most heavily on the people; yet we have
created a military class whose interest traverses that of the people!
. . . The profession of arms has been made honourable; it attracts to
itself thousands of sons and nephews from the more influential families.
The weight of the landed interest, on which, be it remembered, the
ruin produced by war falls more lightly than on the manufacturing
and commercial classes, is thus easily brought to support the military
classes. High priests of the gospel of peace bless the banners of war,
invoke the god of battles—what a devil that god of battles must be
—and pray for the success of their arms in the conflict, while the
people, the long-enduring people, find the money wherewith to pay
the cost, and the common soldiers—poor wretches—are slaughtered
on the horrible field. I ask, 'Are our rulers ready for international
arbitration?' If the question is not regarded as quite beneath their
notice, a considerable section of the press will sneeringly answer 'No'.

I turn to the people and ask, 'Are the people ready?' Let the people declare against war, and where will our rulers obtain the forces to do their fighting? It is indeed a people's question, and the people should earnestly be taught to study it. . . .

It will be said by many, 'This notion of international arbitration is a glorious dream, a fond, an Utopian fancy; to realize it, however, even in part, is impossible'. 'Impossible!' cried the owners of pocket boroughs, and many freemen and the landed interest, when the project was mooted to extend the franchise in boroughs to £10 householders, and to sweep away those provocatives to corruption, the rotten boroughs of England; yet Earl Grey's Reform Bill became law! 'Impossible', exclaimed the judges from their benches, bishops from their thrones and the thousand and one persons implicated in the crime, and interested in the profits, when the abolition of the slave trade and the emancipation of the slaves were proposed: yet, thank God, no slave can now exist where English or American drums sound the roll-call round the world. . . . 'Impossible', declared the landlords and their tenant farmers, and all whom they could cozen, delude or bribe into maintaining their gigantic monopoly, when the nation refused to remain taxed for the benefit of a few; and hungry millions, remembering their fainting and famished wives and children, demanded 'cheap bread': yet the odious corn-laws have been swept away, and we have recently seen the last shilling of duty disappear! Men have proclaimed 'impossible' to the Catholic Emancipation Bill, granting to Catholic citizens equality before the Law, the Municipal Corporation Bill, guaranteeing to the people the right of self-government; the abolition of University tests, nationalizing the higher education, and permitting scholarship to earn the prizes established for scholars, without regard to their views as to sectarian theology; and to the abolition of the vicious and foolish system of promotion in the army by purchase. They have done their best to make such strides on civilization as impossible in fact as they pretended them to be in theory, but the nation rose in the majesty of conviction, in the grandeur of its strength, and both the anachronisms and their defenders sank down before its stately and triumphant march. . . .

. . . There is no such thing as impossible. God has given to men the moulding of all their social institutions, the guiding of their social destiny. He, His Spirit and His angels are on the side of peace-lovers and peace-makers, doubt it who may, the sure promise still stands, men *shall* 'beat swords into ploughshares and their spears into pruning hooks, nation *shall* not lift up sword against nation, neither *shall* they

learn war any more'. The arts of peace shall supersede the arts of war;
the blessings of peace shall supplant the horrors of war; and the fruits
of peace shall reward the sacred toil of mankind!

Reverend John Hyde, *International Arbitration,*
Its Difficulties and Advantages (1873), 20–26

L   The Nonconformist conscience

We learned from a friend, just as the strength of the Nonconformist
feeling against Mr Parnell and his leadership was becoming apparent,
that, in conversation with some Radicals who were in the secrets of
Mr Parnell's friends, he had found that he had fully calculated on the
opposition of the Nonconformists, but thought that it would have little
practical influence. If this were so he has learned by this that he was
just as short-sighted in this as in other matters. Nonconformists can
look upon the part they have played in this melancholy business with
some satisfaction. . . .

We claim no particular credit to Nonconformists for the action they
took, for they could do nothing else without a sacrifice of consistency
and principle. . . . The chief value of the Nonconformist intervention
was that it introduced an element of a distinctly higher character. It
did incalculable service to the cause of Liberalism and progress, and at
the same time it gave practical demonstration of the influence Nonconformists can wield in public affairs, and effectually disposes of the
charge that they would subordinate moral to political considerations.

The events of the last month have changed the whole aspect of
English politics, and must materially affect the cast of our great parties.
There could hardly have been a more striking illustration of the
shallowness of that philosophy which takes no account of the influence
of individuals, but proceeds on the assumption that events are determined solely by the action of great causes, whose force can be accur-
ately measured, and their mode of operation correctly foreshadowed.
Six weeks ago the prospects of a victory for Home Rule were so bright
that it might have been safely predicted that within two or three
years at the furthest, the great experiment, regarded with such hope
on the one side and such anxiety on the other, would certainly be
made. . . . Suddenly the entire situation has been changed, and changed
by the conduct of the one man who had the opportunity of inflicting
an amount of damage upon the cause as was open to no other—so
unprincipled, so unscrupulous, so contemptuous of moral law and of

public opinion, so diabolical in its malignity, so contrary to every dictate of patriotism, and yet so utterly fatuous that even his bitterest foe would not have ventured to hint at its possibility.

. . . English Liberalism will not suffer if Home Rule should cease to be a principal plank in its platform. If that event comes about, not by any faltering in our purpose, or any failure in our policy, but by the deliberate action of the Irish people which renders success impossible, it may prove to be a gain. More disinterested action than that of English Nonconformists and the English democracy generally during the last five years has not many parallels in political history. They have been content to see the reforms on which their hearts were most set thrust aside in favour of a measure whose one recommendation to them was, that it was an act of justice.

. . . During Christmas week its (*The Times*) columns have teemed with attacks upon Nonconformists from correspondents who hide themselves under the mask of anonymity. We regard them simply as tributes to the influence we have been proved to possess. . . . One comment only we will make. If we are guilty of cant in this matter, it is at least without any intelligible motive. Political expediency would have dictated an entirely different course. Our protest might have sent a cleavage right through the Liberal party. Why should we have made it at all if it was a mere piece of Pharisaic pretence? . . .

Our position is very distinct. We adhere to the cause of Home Rule. We espoused it not because we had any admiration for Mr Parnell. We cannot abandon it because he has proved far more unworthy than our worst judgments of him supposed. But we hold that at the present juncture there are interests at stake more vital than any question of Irish government. Mr Gladstone's noble stand has commanded hearty tributes of respect even from opponents. We who have maintained our loyalty to him in former times of difficulty and depression through which we have passed, only honour him the more because of his willingness to forfeit the rewards of his enthusiastic appeals, his arduous toils, and his costly sacrifices rather than compromise the cause of purity and truth.

The Congregational Review, January 1891, 58–69

M   The Social Gospel

The story of the Exodus . . . suggests to us very forcibly the intimate relation of political and social reform to spiritual religion. Religion— pure, devout, aspiring religious life—was not impossible in Egypt. The slave may be a free-souled man, for tyranny has no materials for enchaining the minds and consciences of those who are prepared to bear pain and loss or death rather than be unfaithful. There were children of Abraham's faith in Goshen in the worst days. But taking human nature as it is in the average mass, high, pure, godly living, though not impossible, was not to be expected under such conditions. Some qualities, indeed, could not conceivably be cultivated in a servile race, and the ordinances of an educational religion like that of Moses could not be taught or observed except in a free state. Liberty and healthy conditions could not make men godly. But without exaggerating what liberty could do for the people, these two things are evident—(1) if they were to be healed of those painful bodily diseases which were rife in Egypt, they must be placed where cleanliness and other sanitary conditions were possible; and (2) if they were to be purged from immorality, they must be put in a position to receive instruction, and so far delivered from the oppression of man that they could begin to keep God's precepts without becoming at a bound sublime heroes and martyrs for conscience sake.

The application of these principles is clear. For example, take the case of that hotbed of disease and iniquity in Bethnal Green, which the London County Council recently determined to demolish. If you think, as some are saying, that the Gospel can do nothing for people in such a place as that, you are wrong; the facts are against you. Every room in that space has been constantly visited by members of a neighbouring Christian Church for many years. Dozens, indeed scores, of their tenants have been converted and baptized, while still so destitute that a change of linen had to be provided for them to appear in. Many, very many more, have been socially reclaimed. Yet the district is as bad as ever, and for this reason: directly people want to live a good, clean, sober life, they hasten to escape from such conditions, and other wretched beings take their vacant places. Those who are cleansed by the Word of God come out of such a plague spot. They usually find themselves able to live elsewhere, and they remove. Hence, by moral and religious methods, these physical abominations cannot be destroyed, and so they remain to breed and nourish the social plague. Nothing can rid us of them but a great fire, such as purged London two centuries since, or the strong hand of a political authority razing them to the ground. The London County Council has done well, then, in its resolve, and we do well to encourage and sustain such action on moral and religious grounds. The cost must be enormous. But the money will be well spent. . . .

As churches, we have no political power and no political functions, but as Christian men and women we are under solemn obligation to use every voting power, and every other civic function we possess, to secure the emancipation of the people from those brutalizing conditions under which they so long have lived. . . .

. . . The doctrine that if there were no sin there would be no poverty does not mean that the poor are sinners above all others. Such a notion would be contrary to all intelligent observation of facts, to all the dictates of common sense, and is certainly opposed to the teaching of the Bible. Sin does directly bring millions to want. Idleness, drunkenness, sexual vice, dishonesty, untruthfulness, the lust of pleasure —these things are daily dragging people down from wealth or competence to dire distress. But myriads are born in penury. Thousands are born with such maimed and impaired bodies that work is impossible. Yes, and multitudes are flung into poverty by the sins of their neighbours. Every sinner who goes down drags others into the mire as well, and every transgressor who raises himself for a season by wrong treads others under foot. . . .

. . . There is probably not a church from one end of the land to the other which has not some workers in this field. There is scarcely a class of needy persons, or a form of want which can be named, which some Christian men or women are not trying to meet. The world has no idea of the multitude of beautiful works which are being wrought day and night in England. . . . 'But ye can do them good,' said Christ. What did He mean by good? Did He mean, 'it is in your power to abolish poverty'? No; for it is not. No new land laws, no land nationalization, no multiplication of yeomen, no migrations, no measures of relief, can dig the roots of sin out of humanity. The extermination of poverty will be a blessing which will follow, not precede, the reign of righteousness. But all these works may do some good to men. If they cannot effect all we long to see, they can effect something; and whensoever we will, we can assist such efforts of this class as appear most sagacious and well-planned. . . .

I do not doubt for a moment that the day of renovation will come. I see many and increasing signs of its coming. In the very wails and outcries of despair which fill the air I hear the sounds of that travail of which Paul wrote, and which now has become a widespread and self-conscious birth-pang of a more and more Christian age. In the new activity of national and civic bodies to discourage what is wrong, and to care for men rather than property; in the well-meant though often foolish dreams of social revolutionists, and in the thousand-fold varieties of Christian work—in all these things we may hear at least the rustling of forest leaves which tell that a wind of heaven is blowing, that a sickly calm no longer holds its stifling reign. Yes, a better day is coming. The aspirations and labours of the few are becoming the toil and expectation of the many. The hopes which only lonely prophets dared to entertain in former times are falling like sparks of heavenly fire on many lands, and hearts are kindling everywhere to feel the mercy Moses taught four thousand years ago.

Dr T. V. Tymms in *The Baptist Magazine*,
Volume 84 (1892), 454, 457, 496, 498–500

N   The Collectivist Gospel

Asserting, then, that there is nothing in Christianity against the change [to Collectivism], and assuming that it is not impracticable, I now seek to prove that the Collectivist arrangement has at least four distinguishing merits, demonstrating its closer and stronger affinities with the teaching of Jesus Christ than the present method of administering the physical life of man—(1) It destroys the occasions of many of the evils of modern society; (2) it advances, elevates and ennobles the struggle of life; (3) it offers a better environment for the development of Christ's teaching concerning wealth and brotherhood, and (4) it fosters a higher ideal of human and social worth and well-being. . . .

(i) Collectivism, although it does not change human nature, yet takes away the occasion for many of the evils which now afflict society. It reduces the temptations of life in number and in strength. It means work for everyone and the elimination of the idle, and if the work should not be so exacting, responsible, and therefore not so educative for a few individuals, yet it will go far to answer Browning's prayer:

> O God, make no more giants,
> Elevate the race.

Hesiod teaches that 'Work is the one road to excellence'. 'There is no shame in labour; idleness is shame'. An effortless existence is intolerable, and leads to incalculable mischief. Individualism adds to the number of the indolent year by year; collectivism sets everybody alike to his share of work, and gives to him his share of reward.

As it is necessary to work, so it is useless to steal. Misrepresentation lacks opportunity. Crimes against property are diminished, and become more and more rare. The degradation of women ceases in so far as it is due to want. The problem of the 'unemployed' is solved. And the possibilities of realizing a nobler type of manly life are increased a thousand fold. Surely all this is in perfect harmony with the teaching and spirit of 'Him who came to seek and save that which was lost'. . . .

(ii) Another sign of the closer kinship of Collectivism to the mind of Christ is in the elevation and nobility it gives to the struggle for life. Collectivism does not extinguish combat, but it lifts the struggle into the worthiest spheres, reduces it to a minimum in the lower and animal departments, and so leaves man free for the finer toils of intellect and heart; free 'to seek first the kingdom of God and his justice'. . . . Labour is thus brought into accord with the Greek idea of the state; and, like it, exists 'not for the sake of life, but of a good life'. Are not these results in keeping with 'the mind of Christ'?

(iii) Again, Collectivism affords a better environment for the teaching of Jesus concerning wealth and the ideals of labour and brotherhood. If man is, according to Drummond, only 'the expression of his environment', if, indeed, he is that in any degree, then it is an unspeakable gain to bring that environment into line with the teaching of Jesus Christ.

In the Gospels, accumulated wealth appears as a grave peril to the spiritual life, a menace to the purest aims and noblest ideals. Christ is entirely undazzled by its fascinations, and sees in it a threat against the integrity and progress of his kingdom. 'Lay not up for yourselves treasures on earth'. Jesus frowns on the hoarding of wealth. . . . Now, though Collectivism does not profess to extinguish vice and manufacture saints, it will abolish poverty, reduce the hungry to an imperceptible quantity, and systematically care for the aged poor and for the sick. It will carry forward much of the charitable work left to individual initiative, and, like the London County Council, provide recreation grounds, adding the charms of music for adults, and gymnasia for the children. Again, I ask, is not all that in harmony with the spirit and teaching of Him who bids us see Himself in the hungry and sick, the poor and the criminal?

(iv) Possibly the greatest gain of Collectivism is in its stronger affinity with the high ideals of individual and social life given by Jesus Christ. Collectivism fosters a more Christian conception of industry;

one in which every man is a worker, and each worker does not toil for himself exclusively, but for the necessities, comforts and privileges he shares equally with all members of the community. He works for what we call 'the State' i.e. for the whole of the people of the city and nation in whose prosperity he has a direct interest and whose business is carried on for the welfare of all his fellows, and thereby for himself; succouring the weaker members, aiding the aged and infirm and reclaiming those who are vicious and criminal is part of the duty of a collectivist citizen. . . .

It is a new ideal of life and labour that is most urgently needed. England's present ideal is a creation of hard individualism; and therefore is partial, hollow, unreal and disastrous. But ideals are the main factors in the progress of the home, the parish and the state. They are the forces that move individuals. Individualism fosters the caste feelings and caste divisions of society, creates the serfdom of one class and the indolence of another; makes a large body of submissive, silent, unmanly slaves undergoing grinding toil and continuous anxiety, and a smaller company suffering from debasing indolence and continual weariness; begets hatred and ill-will on the one hand, and scorn and contempt of man on the other. No! the ideal we need and must have is in the unity of English life, in the recognition that man is complete in the State, at once a member of society and of the Government—'a ruler, and yet not ruled'; an ideal that is the *soul* at once of Collectivism and of the revelation of the brotherhood of man in Christ Jesus our Lord, Son of God and Son of Man.

> J. Clifford, *Socialism and the Teaching of Christ*,
> Fabian Society Tract (1897), 6–11

4

NONCONFORMITY AND CULTURE

Nonconformity s attitude to culture may easily be distorted, either by following Matthew Arnold in identifying provincial anti-intellectual Dissent with the whole, or by adopting the equally erroneous equation of Nonconformity with sophisticated Congregationalism and socially and intellectually advanced Unitarianism. Both extremes—and much that lies between them—belong to the Nonconformist tradition, reflecting the continuing tension in the Christian calling between involvement in the world and separation from it.

Throughout the history of Dissent there is an ambiguity here. R. W. Dale was prone to see the Evangelical Revival as the fatal corrosive of Dissenting Culture (**A**), but in truth the Philistine pietist and the political saint already existed as Puritan types before the close of the seventeenth century. Doubtless though, Dale was right in assigning to the agency of the Evangelical Revival a greater tendency to pietism. Certainly the nineteenth century witnessed repeated attempts to direct Nonconformity back to a more positive relationship with culture (**C**(i)). But throughout the period in England, and more especially in Scotland, there was a continuing tradition of faith informed by culture.[1] This point may be illustrated by setting William Hazlitt's estimation of Dissent in his article, *On Court Influence* alongside his earlier, and more often quoted, judgment in *On the Tendency of Sects* (**B**(i) and (ii)).

Robert Vaughan, who did so much to alert mid-nineteenth century Dissent to the richness of the English cultural tradition, argues intelligently on behalf of the culture of the Puritan middle classes *à propos* other social groups (**C**(ii)). As an example of their judgment in action, the *Eclectic Review's* assessment of the Great Exhibition is cited (**D**). There follows a passage from R. W. Dale's rejoinder to Arnold (**E**(i)) which achieved some acclaim, and this is coupled with Unitarian observations on the same theme, which are significant because of Arnold's close association with the Unitarian Rathbone family (**E**(ii)). In both these extracts Vaughan's self confidence has been replaced by a more defensive, hurt apologetic.

[1] For examples of this see:

W. Robertson Nicoll, *My Father: An Aberdeenshire Minister 1812–91*; 1908, esp. chs. I, V–VIII, X & XI.

W. Robertson Nicoll, *'Ian Maclaren': Life of the Rev. John Watson* (1908), esp. pp. 276–7.

T. H. Darlow, *William Robertson Nicoll: Life and Letters* (1925).

Clearly, by the 1870s something was amiss, but Arnold's critique was not the only solvent of that cocksureness which is a main ingredient of the secular dynamic of Puritanism. There was, as the previous section has displayed, the challenge of the submerged tenth which Nonconformists themselves had brought to the surface. Within the chapel communities themselves the perplexing problems of growing wealth and ostentation (**F**(i)) and of the new learning were affecting all but the most socially backward of Nonconformist denominations from the 1860s onwards (**F**(ii)) and different strata of Dissent are shown reacting to these social and cultural pressures in different ways. Spurgeon, the spokesman of all that was toughest in lower middle class and artisan Nonconformity, throws down the gauntlet to the spirit of the age, and the Reverend J. C. Harrison upholds the Puritan ideal of separation from the world (**G**(i)–(iii)).

But perhaps the most valuable reaction to the new social and intellectual climate of later Victorian England was the development of the Institutional Church, which may well be considered a new flowering rather than a perversion of the Puritan spirit which Spurgeon so cherished. Queen's Park Congregational Church, London (**H**(i)) may have been exceptional in the scope and range of its activities, but the autobiographies of numerous Socialist leaders of the present century vouch for the widespread nature of this phenomenon and its vital role in the deepening of the democratic spirit, socially and intellectually, in the formative years of the Labour movement. There was however a reverse side to the Institutional Church: it could rise and then collapse with astonishing speed; in the case of suburban churches it could be the means whereby, through literary guilds and sporting clubs, a middle-class constituency strove to secure the continuing allegiance of its own sons and daughters; more seriously, it could open the back door to secularism (**H**(ii)). The two passages in **I** touch on the kindred problem of the growing pressure of younger Nonconformists for a relaxation of the old Puritan rigours to enable them to indulge in a few harmless pastimes.

Finally, with Matthew Arnold again in mind, upper-class Dissent strove to answer him both effectively and symbolically by frontal assault, by invading the seats of culture themselves; and the admission of Dissenters to Oxford and Cambridge was followed by the establishment of Congregational and Unitarian colleges within the former university. Often enough, cultural aggression lurked only just below the surface of this loudly-trumpeted quest for social justice; the tone of the Reverend R. A. Armstrong's speech in favour of removing Manchester Unitarian college from London to Oxford perhaps explains, if it does not justify, the conviction of Arnold's niece, the authoress Mrs Humphrey Ward, that Dissenters, even liberal ones, would be out of place in the older seats of learning (**J**).

A   The Evangelical Revival and the end of Puritan culture

The Congregational polity is rooted in the great spiritual truth that the ideal Church is so completely one with Christ that it becomes the organ of His will. The Evangelical Revival insisted on the union of the individual saint with Christ; but the union of the Church—an organized society of saints—with Christ was not familiar to it. It cared little for the Church; its whole solicitude was for the rescue of the individual sinner from perdition and the growth in holiness of the individual Christian. It failed to recognize the great place of the Church both in the rescue of men from irreligion and in the discipline of Christian perfection.

The Revival also helped to suppress the original type of Independent character. Reserve, a firm self-restraint in habits of expenditure and in amusements, patient, resolute industry, punctuality in the discharge of all obligations, a family life governed by exact method, a keen interest in theology, and a keen interest in politics, a delight in books and in intellectual pursuits of the severer kind, a strict observance of Sunday —these were the characteristics of the men who had been disciplined by Independent traditions. The great Independents of the Commonwealth who had been formed by other influences were freer and more genial; but in the course of a generation or two the prevailing type of Independent character had taken this austere form. Watts deplored the irregular habits of the Dissenters of his time; but in many Churches the type was still preserved. It was not greatly modified by the Presbyterians who began to enter Congregational Churches in the middle of the eighteenth century; for the Presbyterians who retained the creed of the older Puritans retained also much of their austerity of life. The authority of the original type of character was still asserted by the public opinion of the Churches. Any serious departure from it was condemned.

But when Congregational Churches began to be thronged with Churchmen who had inherited another ideal of Christian morals and conduct, and with still larger numbers of persons who were the children of careless and irreligious parents, and inherited no ideal of Christian morals or conduct of any kind, the whole spirit of the Churches was changed. The moral traditions of Independency were lost. The gravity, severity, and solid strength, to which the habits of an earlier age had formed the members of Congregational Churches, disappeared. The intellectual earnestness also disappeared. Congregationalists ceased to be keen theologians, and they ceased to be keen politicians. During the first twenty or thirty years of this century, the best and noblest men in the Congregational Churches were all aglow with the zeal of the Revival. These men touched the imagination of their contemporaries, and exerted over them the most powerful moral and religious influence; and they created for their successors a new ideal of the Christian life. In the next generation, the ideal Christian man was one who avoided 'worldly' amusements, and freely spent his time and strength in religious work; and among all religious work, evangelistic work had the highest place. By this ideal the Congregational Churches have been governed down to our own time.

> R. W. Dale, *History of English Congregationalism* written before 1894, published posthumously 1907.

B   Two comments from Hazlitt on Dissent

(i)   'On the Tendency of Sects'

There is a natural tendency in sects to narrow the mind.

The extreme stress laid upon differences of minor importance, to the neglect of more general truths and broader views of things, gives an inverted bias to the understanding; and this bias is continually increased by the eagerness of controversy, and captious hostility to the prevailing system. . . . Besides, this perpetual cavilling with the opinions of others, detecting petty flaws in their arguments, calling them to a literal account for their absurdities, and squaring their doctrines by a pragmatical standard of our own, is necessarily adverse to any great enlargement of mind, or original freedom of thought. . . . Hence we may remark a hardness and setness in the ideas of those who have been brought up in this way, an aversion to those finer and more delicate operations of the intellect, of taste and genius, which require greater flexibility and variety of thought, and do not afford the same opportunity for dogmatical assertion and controversial cabal. The distaste of the Puritans, Quakers, etc. to pictures, music, poetry, and the fine arts in general, may be traced to this source as much as to their affected disdain of them, as not sufficiently spiritual and remote from the gross impurity of sense.

We learn from the interest we take in things, and according to the number of things in which we take an interest. . . . A puritanical abhorrence of every thing that does not fall in with our immediate prejudices and customs, must effectually cut us off, not only from a knowledge of the world and of human nature, but of good and evil, of vice and virtue. . . . We can understand the high enthusiasm and religious devotion of monks and anchorites, who gave up the world and its pleasures to dedicate themselves to a sublime contemplation of a future state. But the sect of the Quakers, who have transplanted the maxims of the desert into manufacturing towns and populous cities, who have converted the solitary cells of the religious orders into counting-houses, their beads into ledgers, and keep a regular debtor and creditor account between this world and the next, puzzle us mightily! The Dissenter is not vain, but conceited: that is, he makes up by his own good opinion for the want of the cordial admiration of others. But this often stands their self-love in so good stead that they need not envy their dignified opponents who repose on lawn sleeves and ermine. The unmerited obloquy and dislike to which they are exposed has made them cold and reserved in their intercourse with society. The same cause will account for the dryness and general homeliness of their style. . . .

> *The Examiner*, 10 September 1815. P. P. Howe (ed.), *Complete Works of William Hazlitt* (1930), Volume 4, 47–51.

(ii) 'On Court Influence'

The same consistent writers, and friends of civil and religious liberty, who are delighted with the restoration of the Bourbons, of the Pope, and the Inquisition, have lately made an attempt to run down the Dissenters in this country; and in this they are right. . . . There is some ground for the antipathy of our political changelings to a respectable, useful, and conscientious body of men: and we will here, in discharge of an old debt, say what this ground is. . . . The Dissenter does not change his sentiments with the seasons: he does not suit his conscience to his convenience. . . . The different sects in this country are, or have been, the steadiest supporters of its liberties and laws: they are checks and barriers against the insidious or avowed encroachments of arbitrary power, as effectual and indispensable as any others in the Constitution: they are depositaries of a principle as sacred and somewhat rarer than a devotion to Court-influence—we mean the love of truth. It is hard for any one to be an honest politician who is not born and bred a Dissenter. Nothing else can sufficiently inure and steel a man against the prevailing prejudices of the world, but that habit of mind which arises from non-conformity to its decisions in matters of religion. . . . Dissenters are the safest partisans, and the steadiest friends. Indeed they are almost the only people who have an idea of an abstract attachment to a cause or to individuals, from a sense of fidelity, independently of prosperous or adverse circumstances, and in spite of opposition. . . . Separate from the world, they walked humbly with their God, and lived in thought with those who had borne testimony of a good conscience, with the spirits of just men in all ages. They saw Moses when he slew the Egyptian, and the Prophets who overturned the brazen images; and those who were stoned and sawn asunder. They were with Daniel in the lions' den, and with the three children who passed through the fiery furnace, Meshech, Shadrach and Abednego; they did not crucify Christ twice over, or deny him in their hearts, with St Peter; the Book of Martyrs was open to them; they read the story of William Tell, of John Huss and Jerome of Prague, and the old one-eyed Zisca; they had Neale's *History of the Puritans* by heart, and Calamy's *Account* of the Two Thousand Ejected Ministers, and gave it to their children to read, with the pictures of the polemical Baxter, the silver-tongued Bates, the mild-looking Calamy, and old honest Howe; they believed in Lardner's *Credibility of the Gospel History*: they were deep-read in the works of the *Fratres Poloni*, Pripscovius, Crellius, Gracovius, who sought out truth in texts of Scripture, and grew blind over Hebrew points; their aspiration after liberty was a sigh uttered from the towers, 'time-rent', of the Holy Inquisition; and their zeal for religious toleration was kindled at the fires of Smithfield. Their sympathy was not with the oppressors, but the oppressed. They cherished in their thoughts—and wished to transmit to their posterity —those rights and privileges for asserting which their ancestors had bled on scaffolds, or had pined in dungeons, or in foreign climes. Their creed too was 'Glory to God, peace on earth, good will to man'.

The Yellow Dwarf, 10 January 1818. P. P. Howe (ed.), *Complete Works of William Hazlitt* (1932), Volume 7, 239–42

C Nonconformity and culture in the age of Peel

(i) Dr Vaughan, chairman for 1846, at that time residing in Manchester, had previously been pastor of a Church at Kensington, where he had attracted a number of hearers not often found in Dissenting chapels. As Professor of History in the London University, and as the author of the *Life of Wycliffe* and other important historical works, he had become known in literary circles; and this circumstance attracted many distinguished persons, who listened with pleasure to his preaching. No one could look at him on great occasions without being struck with his appearance and manner. The searching glance from under his knitted brow, his compressed lips, his lordly bearing, his attitude and gesture revealed what was out of the ordinary way, and created expectations rarely disappointed. He took a leading part in the promotion of union between general culture and evangelical religion. Devoted to the latter, he considered that too many of its advocates in earlier days had neglected the study of literature, beyond their own particular domain, and it was his strong conviction that both the piety and the intelligence of Englishmen might be improved by bringing the two things into relation with each other. No one opposed more than he did a subordination of Scripture to the authority of human reason; no one could be more determined to resist an inversion of the order in which the two had ever stood in the orthodox Churches of Christendom.

> Dr John Stoughton[2] *History of Religion in England*, Volume VIII, (2nd edn., 1891), 278

(ii) The charge indeed is sometimes brought against our age, and against congregationalism, and the state of society with which it especially harmonizes in particular, that while there are tendencies in such connexions highly favourable to a certain amount of intelligence, these tendencies are blended with others which are directly hostile to the higher pursuits of learning, to more meditative and profound habits of thought, to everything partaking of the nature of the refined and the beautiful, and which may not be converted into an immediate source of gain.

It must, I think, be admitted that this charge is not without some foundation. . . . No man of sense will pretend that the aristocratic elements of society are without their advantage. There is a nameless grace, dignity and loftiness of purpose which seem like the natural

---

[2] John Stoughton (1807–97) along with Henry Rogers (1806–77), sometime Professor of English Language and Literature at University College, London shared in Vaughan's attempt to effect a marriage between Culture and Evangelicalism; in 1874 on Matthew Arnold's nomination he was elected a member of the Athenaeum.

attributes of high birth and exalted station. There is also an aristocracy in letters and science, to whom the dignity of learned leisure would seem to be every way appropriate and upon whom its influence might be expected to prove in a high degree favourable. But in both these cases the promises and the danger go together. In the history of nations the power to become luxurious has commonly been the precursor to indulgence, corruption and ruin. It is the same with great families as with great nations. The heir to a great house must always have his foot in slippery places. . . . It is the same with the intellectual aristocracy. The power to luxuriate there, also, often proves a temptation much too strong to be resisted; and everywhere facts present themselves, as if for the purpose of showing, that too much independence, and too much leisure, may be as dangerous as too little.

Even in Greece the elite in learning and philosophy would never have had existence apart from the large and intelligent middle class which bore the name of citizens. . . . The culture of the greater number gave existence to a sympathy with the more elevated pursuits of the lesser number, sufficient both to generate and sustain them; and when that atmosphere of sympathy, in which alone the plant could live, had failed, its beauty passed away, and it utterly perished from want of its proper nourishment.

. . . With all this, congregationalism is in perfect accordance. It covets most earnestly popular intelligence, as the soil from which extraordinary minds may be expected most naturally to spring up, and from which alone they can derive permanent sustenance and power. It aims to form intellectual churches; it must in consequence have an intellectual ministry, and it *must*, as a further consequence, have its seminaries of learning to realize that intelligence. It rests nothing upon privilege or prescription, but everything upon truth and reason. . . . This is the spirit of our system and if so, where is the department of knowledge with which it may not be expected to sympathize and intermeddle? It may content itself with average attainment for average purposes; but it does not rest at that point. Its argument depends on a wide range of philology and history, and embraces a multitude of subtle questions relating to social policy and the nature of man—can these things be wisely dealt with by the ignorant, or by the only moderately informed? . . .

We admit that there are some tendencies in modern society, which are not favourable to the higher pursuit of the intellect. It must be confessed, also, that congregationalism has not done all that might have been expected from it, considered as a system in this way; though we think it has done quite as much as could well have been expected from it in the unfavourable circumstances in which it is placed in this country. Religion and society among us have their impression from remote, worldly usage, much more than from the authority of Holy Scripture. Even now, we are the offspring, in nearly all things, of the middle ages, much more than of the New Testament. Congregationalism, accordingly, does not compete with other systems on equal terms. We are severed, both by law and by the action and temper of society, from that alliance with the wealth and power of the land which might serve to develop the capabilities of our system, and to show that everything which the mind of ancient Greece became, in connexion with its freeborn polity, the mind of a Christian nation might become, in connexion with the polity which congregational churches derive from the pages of the gospel. We make no secret of the fact, that we stand in much nearer relation to the popular power of ancient Athens, than to the despotic power of imperial Rome, and we know of nothing in our system inconsistent with any of those higher forms of culture which the latter city adopted from the former.

R. Vaughan, *Congregationalism* (1842), 13–20

D A Nonconformist view of the Great Exhibition

... The realities of the day are represented; and also, its shams. On the one hand, are illustrated, as never before, the whole range of its ever-perfecting machinery, its stupendous locomotives, complex power-looms, spinning-jennies, printing-machines—inanimate witnesses of animate intelligence, embodied symbols of intellect and power; the activity of its textile manufacture, the variety of its pottery and glass, its multiplied material everywhere. On the other hand, is exemplified, thousandfold, the archaeologicalness run wild and rampant of its *art*; the helter-skelter chase after classic, Gothic, Moresque, and almost every other excellence hitherto attained. Smallest attempt at a new one of our own we have, in unguided, unsystematized, *naturalistic*, design—design, that is, too closely mimicking nature, not adequately conventionalizing, in other words, *adaptive* of natural forms to its specific purpose—or, in such puerile anomalies, and base, as *rustic-work* stiffened into cast-iron—a singularly eloquent witness to our opulence in decorative resources. While this humiliating text is enforced through the whole range of manufacturing design, nineteenth-century perfection of copyism, in one characteristic branch, is witnessed in brand-new Gothic crosses and altar-pieces, in mechanical Gothic wood-carving, in more or less tolerable stained glass, and in the 'Mediaeval(*izing*) Court' of Pugin, Hardman, Crace and Minton. The latter, in the strikingly harmonious combination of its stained glass, hardware, wood-carving, hangings, encaustic tiles—all successful repetitions of Gothic models—will at least have the merit of suggesting to many, who would not otherwise have heard of such facts, the fulness of beauty and character, and the homogeneousness, of mediaeval design, however applied, to domestic as to ecclesiastic purposes.

We have a running commentary on the age, its attainments, and shortcomings; and also on the Nations. Here, the changeless *East*, the conditions of whose petrified civilization have preserved the excellences as well as the imperfections of youth, contrasts with changeful Europe. . . .

On the whole, . . . our country makes a noble industrial figure, with its magnificent and suggestive array of powerful and delicate machinery, its similarly unequalled muster of carriages, and agricultural implements, its hardware, its cottons, woollens, silks and other textile goods, its versatile pottery and colossal triumphs in glass. The machinery in *motion* is, above all, a suggestive sight; nor least of all the intelligent-looking operatives that attend it. Earnest labour in their persons makes holiday, gains the privilege of *recognition*, of seeing and being seen by the world at large. Not penned in obscure corners, but in the light of open day, before fine ladies and idle gentlemen, the Manchester factory-girl, or London printer's boy, goes through his accustomed task. Suggestive and noble histrionics these, representing that earnest work-a-day life which makes the world what it is, and not a den of savages. Certainly, as we gaze and listen to these imposing machines, performing their unerring evolutions, it is only of their thoughtful, hard-working inventors, and the hard-working operatives, we think. Or, perhaps, some reflections arise, on the natural blessing machinery was destined to bring the world, in the lightening of labour and facilitation of production, and the large share that has been wrested to a curse, to keeping up *Class*-laws, paying for legitimist wars, and doubling the importance of landed and other labour-proprietors. And fair, indeed, seems that day when labour shall at last reap the harvest which it sows.

For design, the 'Mediaeval Court' already mentioned is, perhaps, the most noticeable feature, in the beauty accruing from well-directed, felicitous copyism. To the same class belong Mr Chubb's locks, with their successful Gothic design; certainly an amendment on no design at all, as used to be the case in such things. Living, self-reliant design, where, indeed, shall we find? The happiest imitation of such original vitality, is but a poor succedaneum. The prevalence of favourite styles of copyism, Gothic, Elizabethan, Louis-Quatorze, which, in decorative art, as in architecture, is the fruit of modern lethargy and corruptions in aesthetics, of having forgotten to maintain an artistic language of our own, is especially prominent on the British side; in its undisguised literalness, unrelieved by continental fancy and vivacity. It is the normal fact, however, among all modern European nations. . . . Compare one of the giant locomotives, where intrinsic necessities have shaped external form, resulting in apparent and essential coherence with nature and fact, with one of those numerous objects wherein a pretence or specious show of art has been made a *mask* in the place of an embodiment of Purpose. How superior aesthetically are the mere reality of the former, the power, the eloquence, the fitness, the simple outlines and harmonious combinations utility has developed, to the poor meretricious make-believe of your rococo side-board with its false outlines, incongruous ornament, or to the dead mechanicalness of the barefaced copy of a Gothic screen. . . .

After all, whether as a work of art, or of industry, the most noticeable English contribution, is the building itself; so imposing a testimony to our resources as a manufacturing nation, so admirably consistent as a (possibly) temporary building, and one erected within the briefest space of time; so appropriate to its purpose, and expressive of it. It obeys Mr Fergusson's canon for a modern building, that it should be constructed fit for its purpose, and trust for aesthetic effect to honesty and fidelity, to unaffected avowal of the ruling conditions of its existence. Certainly, it is the only architectural reality of modern times—the *truest* word spoken in architecture since the days of fourteenth-century Gothic. There is no pretence or disguise. The resources of the material, and of the occasion, are alone relied on. And what a world of commendation is bound up in that one word *Truth*, considering what architecture and nearly all art have so long degenerated into. As whole volumes of falsehood cannot be set at the value of one word of truth, so a whole truthless palace of Westminster is less than a reality like Paxton's. Yet consider the *cost* of falsehood, the cost in superfine material and mechanical ornament, it takes to conceal the want of art and truth; the inexpensiveness of truth itself. Falsehood costs a nation 2,000,000 £; truth, 150,000 £. The one thing is just 150,000 £ better than nothing; the other, two millions *less*, or *worse*, than nothing.

Eclectic Review, June 1851, 739–58

E Matthew Arnold: the Philistine's rejoinder

(i) The more entertaining passages in Mr Arnold's recent animadversations upon us which I had marked for notice must be dismissed with a word. The two main types of Nonconformist provincialism of which he speaks—the 'better type' and the 'smug type'—are they quite unknown among the adherents of the English Church who belong to the same social rank as ourselves? I quite admit that what Joubert says of the Romish services—'Les cérémonies du Catholicisme plient à la politesse;' an aphorism verified in the manners of the common people of all Catholic countries—is true in a measure of the ritual of the English Church; but is not something of the alleged difference between ourselves and churchmen due to the fact that Nonconformity is strongest among the rough and vigorous people of the great towns who live together in masses and whose social habits are not controlled by intercourse with those who inherit the traditions of many generations of culture? And if in villages and small towns there is something more of self-assertion and hardness in the Dissenter than in the Churchman, is not this also partly due to the long exclusion of Dissenters from all free intercourse with the 'gentry', who have had the advantage of university education, of foreign travel, and of the refining influence of the recreations and intellectual pursuits which are at the command of leisure and wealth?

The 'watchful jealousy' of the Establishment with which he reproaches us—whose fault is it? When farmers are refused a renewal of their leases because they are Nonconformists, when the day-school is closed against the child on Monday because it was at the Methodist Sunday School the day before, when in the settlement of great properties it is provided that no site shall be let or sold for a Dissenting chapel, and that if a tenant permits his premises to be used for a Dissenting service, his lease shall be void, can Mr Arnold wonder that we are 'watchful'? Does he think that the uniform conduct of the clergy has been calculated to encourage an unsuspecting confidence in their fairness and generosity? Have we not had reasons enough for maintaining a 'watchful jealousy' against the growth of their power? If sometimes we speak roughly and hastily and bear ourselves ungraciously does all the blame lie with us? It might be more creditable to ourselves and more agreeable to others if we could always 'writhe with grace and groan with melody', but our critics should remember the infirmity of human nature.

R. W. Dale, The Contemporary Review, July
1870

(ii) We cannot linger, tempting as the theme may be, upon the
ingenious nicknames and acrid sneers in which the Apostle of Culture
seems for a time to lose something of that sweet reasonableness on
which he had previously expatiated. For our own part we sympathize
as far as we understand these aspirations with Mr Arnold's warnings
against the extreme forms of Hellenism and Hebraism and in his aim to
unite them in their highest and best forms for our greater human
perfection. In much that he has said there is indeed a warning against
the narrowness and littleness of Dissent which could have had much
weight if it had indicated any due appreciation of the real causes and
deeper characterists of English Nonconformity. Our grounds of separation from the Church are, as it is well known, theological alone; we are
Nonconformists because we cannot conscientiously repeat its creeds or
join in invoking Christ as God. The ordinary grounds of Dissent appear
to us also narrow and unreasonable; but Mr Arnold's tone of arrogant
superiority, his contemptuous indifference to theological opinions, and
his theory of the Church and its Ministry as mere departments of the
state, seem to us to be more fatal to real earnestness of character, and
more injurious to truth, than the narrowest forms of Dissent. While the
cultured man of letters criticizes and scoffs, it is the men strong in the
might of great religious ideals and the spirit of noble enthusiasm who
govern the world.

Review of Arnold's *St. Paul and Protestantism*
in *The Inquirer*, 18 June 1870

F   Other solvents of the Puritan spirit

(i)   *The new wealth*

Hitherto the rich have been a comparatively small and distinct class, and
fashionable society has not been much known at Congregational
churches. Now however there are large numbers of our people who
have become sharers in a greater or less degree in the national wealth,
and who have thereby been brought into contact with a mode of life
with which men in their station would have been strangers in the past.
They have in their new social condition come within the circle of that
mysterious, undefined but powerful organization known as 'Society',
and are expected to conform to its law, commonly called 'fashion'.
Society approves of pleasure, encourages expense, develops a sensitive-
ness to public opinion in matters of dress, of furniture, of food, of

entertainments, and has a wondrous power of exacting obedience to its claims, and as there are in this new age many almost indefinite gradations from wealth to poverty, this mighty social influence is felt over a very wide circle, each grade feeling the influence of that above it, and striving to imitate it in all things as closely as circumstances will permit.

The Reverend R. Wardlaw Thompson in
The Congregational Year Book for 1877, 154

(ii)   *The new learning*

THE ANTI-RELIGIOUS TENDENCIES IN OUR CHURCHES
AND HOW TO DEAL WITH THEM

By an anti-religious tendency we mean any tendency which would degrade things spiritual from their rightful supremacy over things intellectual or social, and material, and prevent or obstruct the free and rapid development of spiritual life in those who constitute a Church. . . .

Among the more thoughtful of those who constitute our membership there is found a taint of Rationalism. We distinguish here between a predominant intellectual appreciation of Christian truth and the sub-ordination of Christian truth to the proud supremacy of intellect. The former is an excellence, the latter is Rationalism. Scientific theories are being broached which, as their authors boast, are opposed to the Mosaic cosmogony. The more intelligent of our members (perhaps not to such an extent in Methodist Churches as in other denominations) are being influenced by these views, not so much because of their individual mastery of them and conviction of their truth, as from the fact that they are endorsed by some of the cleverest intellects of the day. The influence of these views is traceable in a quiet depreciation of spiritual work and workers, in the subordination of things spiritual to things intellectual, political or social, and sometimes in the attribution of very unworthy motives to men who devote their whole time to the ministry of the Gospel. . . .

Inasmuch as some members of our Churches (not many, we hope and believe) take occasion, from their knowledge (whether little or much) of scientific theories, to sneer at everything and everybody religious—inasmuch as, in some quarters, this is considered the proper thing to do in these days of popular science—we think that such foolish conceit and proud ignorance deserve very firm, if not severe, condemnation, both public and private; for it is universally true, whether religion be true or false, and whether science be true or false, that deep humility and dignified reverence should characterize those who undertake to solve the problems of religion or science, or both. Not levity or flippancy, but downright conviction, of the sacredness of things, with action corresponding to it, built up for us the temple of truth, both sacred and scientific. . . .

In our day the great plane of religious conflict is lifted up, for the most part, from the animal to the intellectual nature. Our stiffest battles are now fought not with the low lovers of animal pleasures (the Puritans won on that side), but with the high admirers of intellectuality. Our contention is with men who put their intellectual nature first and who acknowledge no nature superior to it—no spirit possessing inherent supremacy over mind and body. And we must prepare ourselves to affirm with greater boldness the supremacy of the spirit and the great necessity of a Divine inspiration to quicken it into holy life. . . .

By thus maintaining a firm and fearless attitude—by patience and kindliness and tact; by understanding the relative positions and relative claims of philosophy, science and religion—we believe we shall win the battle on the intellectual side, as it has been won on the animal side. In the meantime we are by no means called upon to strike our colours before the blast of the scientific trumpet. Were all the statements of rationalists and scientific men true, they would simply prove that we had misinterpreted in our ignorance a difficult part, or difficult parts of Divine revelation: they would certainly not prove there could be no Divine revelation, nor that the statements of Divine revelation, rightly interpreted, were false; for it is impossible that the Author of nature and the Author of revelation, supposed to be one, and rightly interpreted in both cases, will contradict Himself. . . .

Methodist New Connexion Magazine, Volume 76 (1873), 662–6

G Affirmation of the old virtues

(i) Some persons ask, 'What do you think about dancing?' Well, I never hear the subject mentioned without having an uncomfortable feeling in my throat, for I remember that the first Baptist minister had his head danced off! I am sure I should have to be off my head before I should indulge in that pastime. The usual associations of the ball-room and dancing-parties are of such a character that it is marvellous to me how Christians can ever be found taking pleasure in them. A safe rule to apply to all occupations is—'Can I take the Lord Jesus Christ with me if I go there? If not, it is no place for me as one of his followers.'

Then I may be asked, 'What do you think of games of chance?' Well, I always draw a distinction between games that require the exercise of skill and those that depend largely upon chance as in the shuffling of cards and the throw of the dice. Some games are to be heartily recommended because they tend to sharpen the mental faculties: I do not think the most precise Christian ought to object to draughts or chess—if not played for money—for they help to develop and improve our powers of thought, and calculation, and judgment. Sometimes, when I am weary with my work, I take down my Euclid, and go over a few propositions, or I work out some of Bland's equations, just by way of amusement. That kind of exercise is as much a recreation to me as running out in the fields would be to a boy at school.

In my opinion, games of skill are not objectionable, but every Christian should object to games of chance. Generally, they are played for gain, and hence they excite covetous desires, and so break the tenth commandment. With regard to the great proportion of games of chance we need hardly discuss the question. The time has now arrived when all England ought to be heartily sick of every form of gaming. It used to be a comparatively harmless thing for ladies and gentlemen to spend all the evening over a pack of cards or a box of dice, without any money being at stake; but we have had such practical proof that the worst crimes have sprung from this apparently inoffensive practice, that every Christian mind must revolt from it. Besides, I have always felt that the rattle of the dice in the box would remind me of that game that was played by the soldiers at the foot of Christ's Cross, when they cast lots for His vesture and parted His garments among them. He who sees His Saviour's blood splashed on the dice will never wish to meddle with them.

C. H. Spurgeon, *The Christian's Pleasures,*
A Lecture delivered December 29th 1857

(ii) When the Pastor's College was firmly moulded into shape, we had before us but one object, and that was the glory of God by the preaching of the gospel. To preach with acceptance men, lacking in education, need to be instructed; and therefore our institution set itself further to instruct those whom God had evidently called to preach the gospel, but who laboured under early disadvantages. . . .

Firmly fixing this landmark, we proceeded to sweep away every hindrance to the admissions of fit men. We determined never to refuse a man on account of absolute poverty, but rather to provide him with needful lodging, board and raiment, that he might not be hindered on that account. We also placed the literary qualifications of admission so low that even brethren who could not read have been able to enter, and have been among the most useful of our students in after days. A man of real ability as a speaker, of deep piety, and genuine faith may be, by force of birth and circumstances, deprived of educational advantages, and yet, when helped a little he may develop into a mighty worker for Christ; it would be a serious loss to the Church to deny such a man instruction because it was his misfortune to miss it in his youth. Our College began by inviting men of God to her bosom, whether they were poor and illiterate, or wealthy and educated. We sought for earnest preachers, not for readers of sermons, or makers of philosophical essays. 'Have you won souls for Jesus?' was, and is, our leading enquiry of all applicants. 'If so, then come thou with us, and we will do thee good.' If the brother has any pecuniary means, we feel that he should bear his own charges, and many have done so; but if he cannot contribute a sixpence, he is equally welcome, and is received upon the same footing in all respects. If we can but find men who love Jesus, and love the people, and will seek to bring Jesus and the people together, the College will receive two hundred of such as readily as one, and trust in God for their food; but if men of learning and wealth should come, the College will not accept them unless they prove their calling by power to deliver the truth, and by the blessing of God upon their labours. Our men seek no Collegiate degrees, or classical honours—though many of them could readily attain them; but to preach efficiently, to get at the hearts of the masses, to evangelize the poor—this is the College's ambition and nothing else.

We endeavour to teach the Scriptures, but, as everybody else claims to do the same, and we wish to be known and read of all men, we say distinctly that the theology of the Pastors' College is Puritanic. We know nothing of the new *ologies*, we stand by the old ways. The improvements to be brought forth by what is called 'modern thought' we regard with suspicion, and believe them to be, at best, dilutions of the truth, and most of them old, rustied heresies, tinkered up again, and sent abroad with a new face put upon them, to repeat the mischief they wrought in ages past. We are old-fashioned enough to prefer Manton to Maurice, Charnock to Robertson, and Owen to Voysey. Both our experience and our reading of the Scriptures confirm us in the belief of the unfashionable doctrines of grace; and among us, upon those grand fundamentals, there is no uncertain sound.

> C. H. Spurgeon, *The Autobiography*, com-
> piled by his wife (1899), Volume 2, 148–9

(iii) We are sure of this, that if our churches cease to witness for spiritual life as the basis of fellowship, for separation between the church and the world, and for purity of communion, there is no reason why, as distinct communities, they should continue to exist at all. We therefore hold with all our hearts to the fundamental peculiarity of our churches, and we are persuaded that herein we 'have the mind of Christ'.

> The Reverend J. C. Harrison, *The Congrega-
> tional Year Book* for 1871, 61

H   The Institutional Church

(i)   *In action*

QUEEN'S PARK CONGREGATIONAL CHURCH
Harrow Road, W.
Pastor—Charles Leach.

Large Building Seats 1,500. Institute Seats 650.
Auxiliaries: Sunday Schools—Bible Classes—Band of Hope—Christian Guild—Young Men's Guild—Congregational Guild—Temperance Society—Popular Entertainment—Ladies' Working Party—Savings Bank—Building Society—Medical Society—Sick and Burial Society—Sunday Afternoon Lectures   Week-day Lectures—District Visitors' Society—Cricket Club—Swimming Club—Magazine Fund—Poor Fund.

QUEEN'S PARK INSTITUTE
President—Charles Leach
Principal—G. R. Parkinson, M.C.P.

This Institute has been formed to provide Educational advantages for the inhabitants of Queen's Park and district. The classes are held chiefly in the evening, and at popular prices. Any person of either sex may join one or more of them.

Evening Classes in Music, Languages, Science, Art, Commercial and

Technical Subjects; Preparation for Civil Service, Queen's Scholarships and Certificate Examinations; Book-Keeping, Shorthand, Wood Carving, Clay Modelling etc.

QUEEN'S PARK COLLEGE

A most successful day college for boys and girls.

President—Charles Leach

Principal—Mr. G. R. Parkinson, M.C.P.

of the Royal University: Certificated Teacher of Science and Art: for seven years Master in London and Provincial High-Class Schools.

MASTERS:

Mr A. Robertson, M.A.
Monsieur A. Bruin, Doc.Lit. Hum.
Mr W. Phillips, Fellow of the Tonic Sol-fa College.
Mr J. H. Holloway, Cert. Science Master.
Mr W. S. Hardy, Cert. Science Master.

MISTRESSES:

Miss M. I. Parkinson, C.M. (Queen's Scholar)
Miss L. Champ, A.A. (Oxon)
Miss M. Samuels, A.C.T.C.
Miss A. Leach.

Drill Instructor—Staff Sergeant Young

Fee—One Guinea Per Quarter.

In June last the membership of the various auxiliaries amounted to 2,859. Over 200 persons fill 348 offices, 26 persons receive payment for service, the rest are voluntary helpers. Over 5,000 attendances are made each week in the Winter months.

> The Letter head of the Church notepaper of Queen's Park Congregational Church, London, 1890–91

(ii) *Facing secular pressures*

There are various forms of dissipation which are a serious drawback to the spiritual work of our churches. By the word 'dissipation' we mean that which draws away the energies and time of our members from direct spiritual methods of working, and renders them more or less unfit for spiritual work. . . . In this light many institutions, excellent in themselves, present such temptations to dissipation of energy and time to our members as to seriously interfere with the carrying on of the spiritual life of the Church. Sunday school excursions do so only so far as our members are engaged in Sunday school work: though we should not forget that Sunday school excursions, often accompanied by a band playing dance music among the rest, tend to create in the Church generally a craving for dissipation, for pleasurable excitement for its own sake. Then the Saturday half-holiday has afforded opportunity for all kinds of excursions during the summer half of the year—excursions largely patronized by the working-class portion of our members. From these excursions many of them return home wearied in mind and body at a late hour, sometimes as late as midnight, sometimes beyond midnight, to eat a hearty supper, followed by a heavy, un-refreshing sleep. On the Sabbath morning they rise often too late and always unfit for the holy exercises of the Sabbath School and the sanctuary. . . .

What with one thing and another a minister finds it almost impossible to get a clear fortnight for religious work. If he proposes any plan, and suggests a certain time to carry it out, he is told that the Sunday School Anniversary comes off about that time, and singing must be practised two or three nights a week up to that time. Shortly after the school anniversary, the Young Men's Mutual Improvement Society must hold their annual soirée, to be quickly followed by the school treat, this again to be followed by the chapel anniversary. Then in some districts people begin to prepare for the wakes which are near at hand—a most mischievous element—and our people have no time nor disposition for special religious meetings, and hardly enough for the ordinary. . . .

Interspersed in and between these more prominent events there are penny readings, occasionally at which, among other things, comic literature is read and comic songs are sung; teachers' meetings, monthly or quarterly; Band of Hope meetings, weekly or fortnightly; ladies sewing meetings monthly; with a lecture or concert now and again. . . .

Looking at the whole subject we can see that if there is to be any remedy for this unsatisfactory state of things it must be found somewhere in these two directions—viz, either in a persistent, fearless and united discouragement of everything which does not help forward our spiritual work in some marked degree, or in a knack of making most things serve some spiritual end. The latter method, where possible, is much to be preferred. Our Leaders' Meetings should see to it that our Sunday Schools, our Bands of Hope, our choirs, are servants of the spiritual, ministering to spiritual profit. But some things never can be adapted to spiritual work: these should at once be fearlessly rejected, no matter what the consequences. Our spiritual work, in a spiritual institution like the Church, must be supreme—must be *the* work which all persons and all instrumentalities unite to help forward—nor should we, as ministers of Christ, rest satisfied, nor let others rest satisfied, till spiritual work is supreme.

Methodist New Connexion Magazine, Volume 76 (1873), 714–18

I Permitted pleasures

(i) 'Amusements'. This Topic is one on which the most diverse and antagonistic views are held by religious people. Some hold the most liberal, yea almost lax, opinions on the question, while others regard recreations and diversions as belonging to 'the world', and therefore in a roundabout way to the devil, and as such to be severely left alone. But is there no via media between these extreme views? We think a golden mean can be found in which it will be perfectly safe for us to walk. . . . It is a question of the hour whether Christians ought to go to the theatre. Many good people say 'yes', especially to see the plays of Shakespeare. But why stop at him? He is not the only writer whose histrionic productions are worthy of study. The difficulty of drawing the line is at once seen. . . . Dancing is another question on which many young people would like the church to relax a little of its strictness. . . . Dancing itself need not be wrong: and the sweeping moral objections to it which have often been urged from the pulpit are unpardonable insults to thousands of women who are as pure-minded as any in the country. There may be some dances which good taste and delicate moral feeling disapprove, but so long as high-minded English ladies find pleasure in the ballroom, no one shall persuade me that the offensive and indiscriminate charges which have been flung out against dancing have any truth in them. . . . The Churches, and especially the Sunday School authorities have not given enough attention to the proper provision of pure and healthy amusements for our young people. Why should not a portion of our school premises be utilized on the lines of the Y.M.C.A. for gymnastics, or the quieter games of draughts, chess, bagatelle, dominoes etc.? The church provides no counter-attraction to the world, and while ignoring the social side of her youthful adherents hopes to be able to train them in habits of righteousness. The results of past experience have not been satisfactory, as may be gathered from the fact that the elder scholars have drifted from our care by thousands to join the ranks of those who are either hostile or indifferent to religion.

Primitive Methodist Magazine (1891), 138–41

(ii) 'Nestleton Magna', A Story of Yorkshire Methodism, By Quintus Quarles, Elliot Stock (1876), price 5/-.

A Methodist novel! Alas, and have we not fallen on degenerate times! Would our fathers and founders have written such a book? Would they have tolerated it if written by another? Even two generations ago—aye, we may write, one generation ago—such a book, we fear, would have come under ministerial ban, and been excluded from well-ordered Methodist families. But times have changed, and the sentiments of our predecessors on many subjects are now removed altogether, or held with considerable modifications. We build different chapels—have different singing and preaching in different style, live in different homes and wear different garments to what our forefathers did. Many of our deviations from the primitive type of Methodism are not improvements. We fear they are the result of a growth of worldliness among us, and of a latitudinarianism which comes of an indifference to principle. Even in dress and manners it is well that there should to some degree be a difference between those who fear God and those who fear Him not. To carry about with us an open, tangible evidence that we are on the Lord's side tends to give robustness to our Christian life. We regret for this and other reasons that the garb once distinctive of Methodists has been so utterly discarded by those bearing this formerly despised but now respected, name, and that Methodist congregations are now so fashionably attired as any others to be found either in church or chapel. But many changes are the fruit of culture and increased intelligence; we are less narrow because we are less ignorant, and it is only blind prejudice and unreasoning conservatism that resent the innovation. The founders of Methodism did not altogether ignore our aesthetical nature. To receive pleasure from the sight of beautiful objects, or by the hearing of musical sounds, was not considered by them signs of un-renewed condition.

John Wesley could annotate Shakespeare and give his imprimatur to 'The Fool of Quality', and Charles could cultivate the friendship of the immortal Handel, and be ravished with the celestial strain of his oratorios. The new phase which Methodism is putting on with regard to its recognition of the claims of general literature, and its appreciation of some of its more attractive forms, we contemplate without disapproval and without alarm. Hence the publication of such a book as 'Nestleton Magna', and the introduction of fiction into the pages of the Wesleyan Magazine have nothing portentious in our apprehension. They are signs of the times, it is true, but they indicate, at least such is our hope, that Methodism is going to add beauty to strength, not substitute ornament for stability. As it is not fair that the devil should have the best tunes, neither should these forms of literary composition which fascinate so many minds be restricted to secular themes—Fiction as well as Poetry may be the handmaid of religion.

Methodist New Connexion Magazine, Volume 80 (1877), 243-4

J Cultural aggression

We ought to go to Oxford. If there is indeed that lack of moral earnestness, that lack of an intense desire for truth which characterized our Puritan forefathers and their Puritan ancestors, surely, if we have one spark of the old Puritan spirit left in us today, we should be eager to go there to hold up a light which should not be unworthy of the light our fathers held up. We are told that the new tone of Oxford conversation is, 'Well, it is possible it may be so; and it is possible it may not be so; but it does not matter much whether it is so or not.' Surely then there is no sphere in England which more loudly calls us to go and bear our witness as to what we think of such a tone of conversation. . . . We believe that Oxford as the historic ground of theology affords the happiest atmosphere in which men can study theology. We believe that Oxford whence Wycliffe sent out his 'poor preachers', Oxford where the Wesleys began their work, Oxford the scene of the labours of Cardinal Newman before he joined the Roman Church, Oxford which gave that strange religious inspiration even to the agnosticism and scepticism of Matthew Arnold, Oxford which produced Professor Green—we believe that Oxford is the sphere where theology can be studied with the highest interest and the richest associations drawn from the past. We believe further that even if it should be the will of Providence, as I suppose it will be, that Dr Hatch and Dr Cheyne should pass away, the same temper which has appointed those men to that University will appoint other men of like sort. . . . We are not going in any sectarian spirit for the sake of preaching any particular dogmas, dear to us as the particular dogmas may be. We are going that we may set the example of free teaching and free learning in theology. Should free teaching and free learning in theology be recognized in the great religious centre of English life, or should they not? If we are not going to proclaim them, then who is? Can a Broad Church proclaim them? There is no community in this country save ours that ever can or will carry to Oxford that noble spirit of free learning and free teaching which we have inherited, and to which our faithful teachers have devoted their lives. Sir, to my mind, the most formidable argument advanced against the Oxford move is that which one or two speakers, especially Dr Martineau have advanced, namely the lack of opportunity for practical missionary work. I have tried to look at this thing straight, with the memory of my own student days in my mind and with a very considerable knowledge of the young men who have come out of the College since I was one of its students, and I believe, Sir, that we may sometimes lay too heavy a weight upon those young spirits, if at the very same time they are taxing their intellects by the highest efforts which they can make, we ask them to go and labour in the purlieus of East London, to witness the misery and try to solve the social problems of our day. . . . Now I want to send these young men where a game of cricket or a pull on the river shall not be a thing to be stolen, but a thing to be freely enjoyed. . . . Those who are to listen to their preaching—or their praying—afterwards will not, I think, Sir, be the sufferers, if for a little while they are allowed to defer those terrible toils among the poor and suffering, and are allowed to spend their young lives in a brighter atmosphere, tempering the labour of mental study by those things which God meant to make young men's lives glad.

> Speech of the Reverend R. A. Armstrong, advocating the removal of Unitarian theological training from London to Oxford, reported in *The Inquirer*, 14 July 1888

5

NONCONFORMITY AND
THE STATE

With the repeal of the Test and Corporations Acts in 1828, the last obstacles in the way of Nonconformist political enfranchisement seemed to have been removed. The *Evangelical Magazine*, voicing the attitudes of the London leadership of Dissent (**A**) waxed almost lyrical in its gratitude to the Wellington government, the Lords Spiritual and Temporal and King George IV. This complacency was resented by provincial Dissenters, especially the socially unprivileged, and the reasons for their distrust as well as the real limits of religious toleration that they still endured are revealed in Joseph Ritson's account of the sufferings of the early Primitive Methodist itinerants (**B**). The fewer these disabilities became, the more unbearable were those that remained —in consequence much of the history of nineteenth-century Dissent is taken up with campaigns for the recognition of the validity of their own domestic rites in the celebration of the great facts of human experience, birth, marriage and death; a generation-long battle against church rates; and an assault upon those fundamental bastions of the Anglican establishment—the ancient universities—leading up to the University Test Acts of 1854, 1856 and 1871.

It was provincial Dissent, especially that of the northern counties, which took the lead in a campaign of opposition to the established church, but this was very much a consequence of the Repeal, and the advent of the reforming Whig government of 1830–41. Till then, as the extract from Robert Hall (**C**) makes clear, Dissenters had for the most part been content to remain 'quiet in the land'. Thereafter, emboldened by their growing numbers and social prestige, Dissenters through the Anti-State Church Association, later the Liberation Society, waged a vigorous campaign for the disestablishment of the National Church. Edward Miall MP, a Congregationalist, was the acknowledged leader of this movement inside and outside parliament. The personal animus which he bore towards the Anglican Church is reflected most especially in his *Nonconformist's Sketchbook* (**D**); in their official resolutions the Dissenting bodies tended to be far more restrained (**E**). This is not to say that they were not conscientious and whole-hearted in their hostility to the establishment principle: both with regard to Catholic Emancipation in 1829, to the Maynooth Question in 1845 and Papal Aggression five years later there was concern that a spirit of pan-Protestantism should not obscure an essential voluntaryism

which, in part at least, had common cause with Catholics as fellow Dissenters.
Similarly the *Regium Donum*, whereby £1,695 of crown funds was employed
for the relief of necessitous ministers and their widows, was suspended in 1852
on the petition of Dissenters who were fearful that their voluntaryism was
thereby compromised. That Miall's campaign marked a decisive shift away
from a demand for constitutional liberty to one for social equality was recognized by the usually percipient Unitarians. Extract **F** underlines emphatically
the type of rather mean-spirited social egalitarianism for which some Dissenters were striving. As the possibility of Disestablishment became more and
more remote from the mid-70s onwards, more thoughtful Nonconformists
began to shy away from the consequences of their demands: Joseph Parker's
novel 'Weaver Stephen' (**G**) marks a significant change of heart.

Voluntaryism in education is the complement of political laissez-faire and
the quest for religious equality. The case for the churches to be left alone by
the state in order to educate the nation's children themselves was expressed
vigorously from the 1830s onwards, especially after the failure of the attempted
'Anglican aggression' of Sir James Graham's Factory Bill of 1843. In extract
H Edward Baines argues comprehensively on moral, political, social and
religious grounds for the Voluntary Principle. By the late 1860s however,
when even the staunchest Dissenters were compelled to admit that Voluntaryism had failed to educate all but a fraction of the nation's poor, and were
excusing their own paltry efforts by pointing to the numbers of sunday schools
founded, chapels built and foreign missions established, Nonconformity per-
petrated its most astounding volte-face of the century, and plumped for state-
sponsored secular education (with of course a degree of local control). This
required some very special pleading or else a frank admission of inconsistency
(**I**). Not all Dissenters welcomed this move, or the epithet 'secularizing' with
which they could now justifiably be branded. Spurgeon and his vast conservative evangelical following had their reservations (**J**), while the Wesleyans
who strove to retain and extend their own denominational schools tended to
side rather with the Roman and Anglican opposition to 'godless' education.
Such arguments as those used by the Reverend Charles Garrett (**K**) only
reinforced the Dissenters' traditional distrust of Wesleyan 'priestcraft'.

The last two extracts relate Nonconformity to wider political issues:
R. W. Dale points to the consequences of the 1867 franchise reform in
terms of education and municipal action; Joseph Chamberlain also writing
from Birmingham indicates that the writing is on the wall for the alliance
between the Liberal Party and the Nonconformists unless the latter give more
serious attention to working class needs (**L** and **M**)

A   The end of the Test and Corporation Acts

The friends of Religious Liberty throughout the country have, ere this time, enjoyed the high satisfaction of knowing that these miserable relics of a persecuting age have been obliterated from the Statute Book of this free country. . . . To the *Executive Government*, the Rt. Rev. *Prelates* of the English Church, Lord *John Russell*, and Lord *Holland*, and, indeed, to both Houses of Parliament, the Protestant Dissenters are deeply indebted, and doubtless feel themselves very grateful. But let them not forget that *to their own principles* they are most of all indebted, and that by a perseverance in them, they cannot fail to maintain and augment their privileges. . . .

On Wednesday, June the 18th, upwards of 400 individuals dined at Freemasons' Hall, for the purpose of marking, with sufficient distinctness, the sense which Dissenters and others entertain of the value of the late concession of Parliament in favour of the great principle of religious liberty. His Royal Highness the Duke of Sussex presided, and a numerous circle of Peers and Members of Parliament honoured the festivities with their attendance. Several appropriate toasts were drunk with demonstrations of lively joy, amongst which we were glad to learn that one related to the liberal and enlightened conduct of the Bishops. Though the meeting was kept up to a late hour, all was orderly and dignified to the last. There were no songs, nor unbecoming convivialities.

Evangelical Magazine, Volume 6 (N.S.) (1828), 259, 311

B   Continuing disabilities

But the severest trial was to be called upon to contend with rowdy opposition and positive violence when exhausted by long and hungry journeys. The less brutal form of opposition was a mere attempt to drown the singing and preaching by noise. The noise varied, from the ringing of the church bells—so violently that they were sometimes actually cracked—and the rattling of tin pans and kettles, to the beating of drums, the blowing of horns, and the noise and clamour of a dog fight. But the opposition often took a far more aggressive form. Mobs have always been fond of throwing missiles. In the early days stones were generally plentiful and handy, and at

Lincoln, William Clowes was wounded with one. But occasionally a little variety was introduced. Thus, at Market Rasen, shot was slung. At Faringdon Thomas Russell and his helpers were pelted with potatoes. . . .

But the favourite missiles were rotten eggs, so finely expressive of hatred and contempt. In one day Thomas Russell was so besmeared with rotten eggs and filth that he thrice sat down by the side of the canal or brook or pond, and, taking off his clothes, washed them. Resuming his wet garments, he continued his mission in another place. . . .

Another missionary, George Wallis, was in Hampshire drenched with bullock's blood; and at Belper the redoubtable John Benton narrowly escaped the same fate. His assailant slipped upon the ladder he had ascended, and the blood intended for Benton was precipitated upon himself. These cases are only typical of what took place in various parts of the country.

But instances were not wanting of physical violence with murderous intent. At Stow, in 1819, John Garner was driven out of the village, after standing a seige for some time in a house where he had intended to preach, and pelted with stones, rotten eggs and filth. Then he was seized, and, while his mouth was held open, attempts were made to pour sludge down his throat. 'Kill the devil' was the cry, and immediately he was knocked down, kicked and beaten, and dragged to a pond where it was the evident intention of the mob to drown him. At this moment of peril he was strangely enough rescued by one of the vilest of his persecutors and escaped. The garments torn violently from his person were so ragged and tattered that they afterwards served as a scarecrow in one of the village gardens. . . .

But more cruel than any of these methods of persecution was that of boycotting, though the name had not then been invented. All over the land were men and women who were made to feel that religious liberty, in the true sense, did not exist. To countenance or harbour the Primitive Methodist was to risk the displeasure of their social superiors: the squire, the parson, and perhaps the farmer. To hazard that was to hazard their employment and their home, and sundry pains and penalties which petty tyrants know so well how to inflict. To keep this new and aggressive form of Dissent out of the parish, it was deemed necessary to prohibit anyone from allowing services to be held in his house. The man who disregarded the prohibition was evicted. Even to shelter the missionary or give him hospitality was to risk the loss of employment. In hundreds of cases the screw was mercilessly applied in this way to labourers and even to tenant farmers. The very shopkeepers joined the boycott in the case of Thomas Proctor of Cwm, refusing to sell him food, and for days his chief sustenance was only what he could gather off the hedges. In Berkshire the preachers sometimes had to wander on the Downs all night, after preaching, having nowhere to sleep. In some cases the people were forbidden even to look out of their doors or windows when the missionary visited the village. . . . The present generation has no idea of the lengths to which religious intolerance and persecution went in the days of our fathers . . . in about a score of instances the missionaries on various charges, often of the most flimsy character, were convicted and imprisoned. . . .

As early as 1821, we find Mr Thomas Waller, a cotton spinner, committed to prison for three months simply for preaching in the streets of Ashton-under-Lyne. Probably Jeremiah Gilbert had the largest experience of this kind. In fifteen months he was taken before the magistrates no fewer than fifteen times, as he himself records, in June 1820, for preaching the Gospel. At Eckington in Derbyshire, standing on a chair, he was conducting a service, when the constable desired him to come down. Thrice Gilbert asked for the summons, and when it was not forthcoming, went on with his sermon. The constable then called for assistance, but nobody responded. He then seized the preacher by the coat and pulled him down. Taking the constable's arm, Gilbert began to sing: 'Christ, He sits on Zion's hill', and marched off to gaol. Looking through the bars of the prison, Gilbert perceived a crowd of people assembled, and exhorted them to flee from the wrath to come. Then he sang the praises of God within, while the people sang them outside the gaol. 'After some time the gaoler came in', he records, 'and conversed with me. I persuaded him to go down on his knees in the prison and prayed with him. I afterwards wrote a part of my Journal, and at midnight I prayed and sang praises to God, and then retired to rest. I had blocked up the wndow as well as I could to keep out the cold, for it was a wet, damp, doleful prison. I had neither bed nor straw, but lay across some laths, and had a besom for my pillow. It was afterwards remarked to me that my prison was a deal worse than Derby dungeon; but the Lord converted it into a paradise.'

J. Ritson, The Romance of Primitive Methodism (1909), 165–73

C 'Quiet in the land'

From the time of Queen Elizabeth under whom they (the Puritans) began to make their appearance, their views of religious liberty have gradually extended, commencing at first with a disapprobation of certain rites and ceremonies, the remains of papal superstition. Their total separation from the Church did not take place for more than a century later, till, despairing of seeing it enacted on a comprehensive plan, and being moreover persecuted for their difference of sentiment, they were compelled at last reluctantly to withdraw. Having thus been directed by a train of events into the right path, they pushed their principles to their legitimate consequences, and began to discern the impropriety of all religious establishments whatever, a sentiment in which they are now nearly united. On this very account however, of all men they are least likely to disturb the peace of society, for they claim no other liberty than what they wish the whole human race to possess, that of deciding on every question where conscience is concerned. It is sufferance they plead for, not establishment; protection, not splendour. A disposition to impose their religion on others cannot be suspected in men whose distinguishing religious tenet is the disavowal of all human authority. . . .

The prejudice entertained against us is not the work of a day, but the accumulation of ages, flowing from the fixed antipathy of a numerous and powerful order of men, distributed through all classes of society; nor is it easy to conceive to what a pitch popular resentment may be influenced by artful management and contrivance. Our situation in this respect bears a near resemblance to that of primitive Christians against whom, though in themselves the most inoffensive of mankind, the malice of the populace was directed, to a still greater degree, by similar acts and upon similar principles. The clamour of the fanatic rabble, the devout execration of Dissenters, will remind the reader of ecclesiastical history of the excesses of pagan ferocity, when the people, instigated by their priests, were wont to exclaim, 'Christianos ad leones'. There is the less hope of this animosity being allayed, from its having arisen from *permanent causes*. That Christianity is a simple institution, unallied to worldly power; that a church is a voluntary society, invested with a right to choose its own officers, and acknowledging no head but Jesus Christ; that ministers are brethren, whose emolument should be confined to the voluntary contributions of the people; are maxims drawn from so high an authority, that it may well be apprehended that the Church is doomed to vanish before them.

Under these circumstances, whatever portion of talents or of worth Dissenters may possess, serves only to render them more hated because more formidable.

[Dissenters will be] happy if the frowns of the world should be the means of reviving that Evangelical piety which once distinguished them so highly. Content if they can gain protection ,without being so romantic as to aspire to praise, they will continue firm, I doubt not, in those principles which they have hitherto acted on, unseduced by rewards, and unshaken by dangers. From the passions of their enemies, they will appeal to the judgment of posterity—a more important tribunal. Above all, they will calmly await the decision of the Great Judge, before whom both they and their enemies must appear, when the springs and sources of their mutual animosity will be laid open; when the clouds of misrepresentation being scattered, it will be seen they are a virtuous and oppressed people, who are treading, though with unequal steps, in the path of those illustrious prophets, apostles and martyrs of whom the world was not worthy. In the mean time they are far from envying the popularity and applause which may be acquired in a contrary course; esteeming the reproaches of freedom above the splendours of servitude.

R. Hall, *An Apology for the Freedom of the Press and For General Liberty* (Seventh edn., 1822), 72–87

D   'Our strength lies in aggression'

To do or to be anything on sufferance is degrading if it involves our own acquiescence in inferiority. We cannot escape from the feeling that our position is one of unmixed littleness. We are *endured*, and therefore there is no scope for our assertion of inalienable right—we are *only* endured, and this cannot consist with cheerful self-respect. What is the inevitable consequence? All around us there exists a stagnant and oppresive atmosphere of contempt. The point on which we stand does not lift us above it. We cannot escape it—we breathe it daily. In the primitive age of Christianity, at the Reformation, and during the years of puritan persecution, the moral heroism of the devout elevated them far above simple derision. With us, moral heroism is impossible, and we go about the world with a label on our backs, on which nothing more is written than the word 'Fool'. Nobody hinders us, we may walk where we please—but the brand is upon us, and we cannot forget it. We become ashamed of ourselves—ashamed of our principles—and look and speak and act, as though we were ordained to be despised, and have made our calling sure. . . .

We want the decision, without the violence, of the first reformers. Our strength lies in aggression, rather than in defence. The system which at present obstructs the free working of Christian principles, and the general diffusion of Christian truth, must be smitten with the sword of sharp rebuke, and pursued with all the determination of purpose which should sustain the minds, and brace up the energies, of men who are aiming at the overthrow of antichrist. Whatever there is of real good, mingled with the mass of corruption and evil, will survive the system which it now helps to sanctify, and by which its own elasticity and usefulness are well nigh destroyed. Upon all national churches is enstamped, in deep and indelible characters, the mark of the beast. All kind of alliance with them, the genius of Christianity strictly prohibits. 'Come out and be separate' is the only command which, in reference to these institutions, we are permitted to regard. Homage, even the most indirect, paid to the state church is, in essence, the recognition of falsehood and the worship of a lie.

E. Miall, *The Nonconformist's Sketch Book* (1842), 197, 280

E   Disestablishment resolution

Resolution passed by the Lancashire and Cheshire Association of Baptist Churches

That this Union avails itself of its annual session again to record its deep conviction of the unscriptural character of the established churches of this country. Believing all such institutions to have had their origin in the apostacy which took place shortly after the death of the apostles of our Lord, to be repugnant in their nature to the spirituality of the Saviour's kingdom, and to be a fruitful source of social wrong, religious formality and national scepticism, the brethren assembled feel bound to protest against their continuance. That these views are confirmed by the clearer development of church principles recently furnished by a large and rapidly extending portion of the clergy, a development the more singular and opportune as occurring just at a moment when public attention was specially directed to the constitution and working of the English Church. Believing such views to be the legitimate growth of the principles on which the English hierarchy is founded, and re-garding them, at the same time, as subversive of the spirituality of the gospel, and fatal to the souls of men, this Union, as an assemblage of religious men, recognizes the obligation under which it is placed, strenuously to exert itself for the disestablishment of the English Church, from the secular associations into which it has been forced. That such exertion is regarded as a religious duty, devolved upon them by the terms of their Christian profession, and imperatively demanded by a due regard to the religious welfare of their fellow men.

> Manuscript Minutes, Lancashire and Cheshire
> Association of Baptist Churches, Thursday,
> 21 May 1842

F   Liberty or equality?

We may confine ourselves to the allegation that we have all the religious liberty we need. But is this the case? Have we Nonconformists all the liberty we need, when one of our ministers cannot conduct service in a church, however warmly invited by the clergyman, without being liable to an indictment for brawling in church? Have we all the liberty we need when no one of our ministers, however widely respected, could be nominated to the chaplaincy of a gaol, or even of a regiment of Volunteers? These are, indeed, small matters. True, so the church-rate grievance seemed to those who remembered the disabilities of the Test and Corporation Acts. But if small in themselves, they touch closely upon what is in reality the greatest matter of all, viz: the inequality which is still kept up by the maintenance of the connection between 'Church and State'. We thought that the day had gone by when Dissenters were content with 'toleration' and the possessions of 'liberty'. Was it not at the last Provincial Assembly that the sentiment 'civil and religious equality' was substituted for the humbler 'claim of civil and religious liberty', and that amid general applause? Is this right, or is it wrong? Is it a mistake to believe that the fair working out of a people's religious life can never be secured until every form of organization which it may assume shall not only be permitted, but shall stand absolutely equal before the law? It is this principle that is violated by the state-upheld predominance of a single sect out of all the varieties of religious belief and ecclesiastical forms in which the religious life of England embodies itself. That predominance is, we believe, as mischievous for the sect elevated as for those which are subordinated. To this latter mischief, Dr Bellows bore significant testimony when, on his return to America, he spoke of the whole Nonconformist life and

activity of England striking him as constantly labouring under a subdued sense of being over-shadowed and sat upon, lacking the manly
independence which characterizes the same bodies in America. We
acknowledged at the time that there was great justice in his remarks.
The Establishment with its vast power of quiet repression and discouragement acts as a great wet-blanket upon the free religious impulses even
of that half of society with which it has nominally no connection. Nor
is it less mischievous upon the Church itself. The vast religious power
of that Church is 'crabbed, cabined and confined' by the exigencies of
that very subordination to the secular government on which it, in its
folly, prides itself. Look where you will through the organizations and
institutions of the Church, and every element that comes of its *establishment* is an element of weakness; forms that breed contention; creeds
that engender doubt, not faith; the sale of livings, a scandal such as
Catholicism does not tolerate; and the shameful prayers for the guid-
ance of the Holy Ghost to choose the one bishop already appointed by
the Prime Minister of the day! On the other hand, look at the real
religious power and activity of the Church. We gladly admit all that it
has done and is doing. But this is the outcome of voluntary effort.
What has repaired the old churches, and built new ones? What has sent
forth the army of Scripture-readers? What is calling forth the orders of
lay-helpers? The element of voluntaryism in the Church. Here is the
significance of the name of the Society. It is not Dissenters whom we
want to 'liberate'. We want to liberate religion. We want to liberate
the Church of England from that 'state patronage and control' which
only fosters indolence and pride, and on free religious life as an incubus
and a restraint.

As to what might eventually become of the Church revenues, we
regard that merely as a secondary and collateral consideration. The only
thing that is evident is that (except, perhaps, those that have accrued
since 1662) they are national property, and that as national property
they must be dealt with. Mr Green objects to their being appropriated
to any but 'religious and charitable uses'. Well and good; so do we, and
if ever the time comes, we have little doubt that 'religious and charitable uses' can be found for whatever available surplus there may be.
On two points however, we have *no* doubts. No method of dealing
with the Church's property that the wildest member of the Liberation
Society has ever broached, would be such an 'invasion' or 'spoilation'
as was that by which the Protestants came into possession of it at the
Reformation. And, no purposes to which it could be put could possibly
be less 'charitable or religious' than that to which at present a large

proportion of it is put. For 'religious' uses let the disposition of the vast
cathedral revenues be studied. Let its innumerable doles and gifts,
applied almost exclusively to the smallest sectarian proselytism, answer
for the Church idea of 'charitable purpose'.

> *Unitarian Herald*, 9 December 1870. A Leader
> in reply to a letter from the Reverend Henry
> Green of Knutsford, a critic of the Liberation
> Society and admirer of the Established Church

G   Dissenters against Disestablishment?

To hear Paterson upon the great question of Dissent, you would suppose that he was the most violent and despotic of men, a red-handed
revolutionist, and a very desperado. His controversial epithets were
forged in the fire of his personal contentiousness. He had no idea that
he was using strong language when he denounced the clergy as dumb
dogs that cannot bark, curates as mumbling puppies not fit to be at
large by themselves, patrons as jobbers in the souls of men, and bishops
as overfed old women who neither understood the spirit of the age,
nor grasped the purpose of the kingdom of heaven. All this was quite
in harmony with my friends' conception of Christian charity. . . . .

Paterson had just returned from a 'monster demonstration' in favour
of free church principles and left the Establishment with not an argu-
mentative leg to stand on. The demonstrators had cheered until they
were hoarse, and waved their handkerchiefs for minutes together in
wildest delight. The bishops had been eloquently described as white
robed self-seekers (vehement cheering), the steeple-house had been
described as the half-way inn on the road to Rome (tremendous
applause), and the sale of livings had been denounced, with some in-
distinctness of meaning, as the 'saturnalia of the pit' (vociferous cheering in round after round, the women waving their parasols, and men
throwing up their hats in the air). The whole 'demonstration' gave
immense encouragement to the Nonconformists, and led them to
think that it might have an important influence upon 'the government
of the day'. Paterson had been a leading speaker in the 'demonstration',
and had produced a tremendous effect upon his own throat, as was
proved by a most rasping hoarseness. Paterson's travelling expenses to
the scene of tumult had come to thirteen and sixpence, and after being
examined how he made them so much, the organizers gave him half a
guinea, and a vote of thanks. But nothing could daunt the valiant
Paterson. . . .

Paterson speaks: 'There is no flaw or crack in my Dissent. I go on all fours, and I go straight on, no matter who or what is in my way. My opinion is that the Church will be disestablished in about five years.'

Whiteman smiled. 'Not in fifty years,' said he. 'You make a grievous mistake about Dissent. If the archbishops themselves were to say to you, "Paterson, draw up a scheme for Disestablishment that shall be honest and right in all directions," I should, on hearing their proposals, instantly defy you to carry out their wishes.'

'Why not?'

'Simply because the question is the most complex one in the whole political sphere. It is not a question of Disestablishment only, but of Disendowment, and that means the equitable distribution of an infinite amount of property. I wish to tell you, Paterson, that there are Dissenters who are not of your temper; there are men who are unwilling that St Paul's Cathedral should be turned into a cattle market, or that Westminster Abbey should be turned into a railway terminus.'

'Is there anything wrong then in a cattle market or a railway terminus?' Paterson bluntly enquired.

'Not at all,' Whiteman replied. 'They are both right in their own place. After all, you cannot take out of life the subtle influence of sentiment; you may laugh at it, you may underrate it, you may call those who are subject more largely than others to its influence superstitions and fanatical; but as a matter of fact there is in this nation a sentiment which will not allow the Cathedrals of England, its great ministers and its noble churches, to be secularized or degraded.'

J. Parker, *Weaver Stephen* (1886), 118, 127, 283-4

H Voluntaryism

Let me first define what is meant by the Voluntary system. It seems needful to inform some that it is not confined to charity; still less does it mean Dissent. The Voluntary system includes all that is not Governmental or compulsory—all that men do for themselves, their neighbours or their posterity of their own free will. It comprehends the efforts of parents, on behalf of the education of their children—of the private schoolmaster and tutor, for their individual interest—of religious bodies, benevolent societies, wealthy benefactors and cooperative associations, in support of schools—and of those numerous auxiliaries to education, the authors and editors of educational works, lecturers, artists, and whoever devotes his talents in any way to promote the instruction of the young, without the compulsion of law, or the support of the public purse. He who has imagined that the Voluntary system implies anything less than this, has been under a strange delusion. He who understands its import sees that it rests on the broad basis of parental duty and affection, and of the intelligence, patriotism and religion of the people, aided by the competition of all the educators who press forward to supply a universal want.

Whilst the Voluntary system enlists in its aid these natural and noble agencies, its very essence is *liberty*. It offends no man's conscience, exacts from no man's purse, favours no sect or party, neither enforces nor forbids religion in the schools, is open to all improvement, denies to no person the right of teaching, and gives to none the slightest ground of complaint. It is as just and impartial as it is free. . . . A system of education resting on the Government or on compulsory taxation, is at variance with the genius of our institutions and national character, and, if carried out as the principle would require, and applied to the press and pulpit, to literature and science, would degrade the English nation into a resemblance of Continental nations, in which the bureaucratic system has annihilated the noble spirit of self-reliance, and with it the best safeguard of public liberty. . . .

To the Government and Parliament I would humbly say—Throw the people on their own resources in Education, as you did in Industry; and be assured that, in a nation so full of intelligence and spirit, Freedom and Competition will give the same stimulus to improvement in our schools, as they have done in our manufactures, our husbandry, our shipping and our commerce. . . .

In the arguments for Government education there is a strange ignoring of one of the great excellencies of the Voluntary system, namely, its effect in knitting together the different classes of society. Every operation of that system brings those who take part in the support of schools into contact with parents or children of a class different from their own sort, and thus exercises the sympathies of each class towards the other. For example, in the Sunday Schools of England we have three hundred thousand gratuitous teachers, who not only instruct the children in school, but often visit them in their homes, reclaim them from their wanderings, provide them with books, bring them into Temperance and other societies, counsel them, pray for and with them, and anxiously watch over their best interests. Can this be, without exercising a most important influence both over the teachers and the taught; or without acting as a cement between the ranks of society to which they respectively belong? Impossible. I speak from long observation when I say, that the blessings to both classes are beyond our power to estimate. In like manner, every educational committee in the Kingdom, with its visitors of schools and homes, is a centre of influence, from which is spun, so to speak, a beautiful web of social affections, which none but the utterly thoughtless can fail to admire and prize. Now Government education would destroy all this admirable organization. . . .

Answers to the objections urged against the Voluntary system are perfectly satisfactory. The apparent force of any of the objections arises from taking a partial view of the vast and varied agencies embraced in the Voluntary system. Look fairly at the whole, and they will be found equal to the requirements of our social want. To conclude otherwise sems to me a reflection on our Maker himself, whom it would convict of leaving his creation and providence defective in one of its most essential points. He has endowed his creature, Man, with the instincts and the reason which qualify him for his own support and the care of his offspring as to their animal wants: and can we believe that He has left out of that wondrous organization the springs which would move men to provide for the higher and immortal nature of their children? True, He has permitted Sin to invade our world, with a horrid brood of evils, darkening our moral nature. But there still remains, among the least impaired of our right affections, parental love: and He has provided the grand restorative of human virtue, the Gospel of His Son, with principles so heavenly as in their natural working to repair the ruin of the Fall. There exist then, natural means in society for the moral training of the rising race. Even were it not so, the governments created by men would be at least as indifferent as the men themselves to that work. But those means will be the more powerful the more they are directly employed. Civil government is no fit agency for the training of families or of souls. It has neither the motive nor the adaptation for such a duty. . . .

Now under the Voluntary system the religious element, which I maintain to be the most important in education, may be naturally introduced, without offence to conscience. It is not made the subject of legislative requirement; it is not supported by public taxation; it is not imposed on anyone. Creeds and catechisms are not essential to the system, though they need to be prohibited; God's own book, in the hands of a pious teacher, is all-sufficient. The school may be opened with prayer and the reading of the Bible. Scripture history may be taught, with a free deduction of the religious lessons in which it abounds. Every branch of instruction may be conducted, and all discipline maintained, in a Christian spirit, and with a constant recollection of the highest interests of the children; and the teacher will never feel himself fettered. We may thus, under the Voluntary system, have the full benefits of *Religion* and *Freedom*, and under no State system can they be combined.

> E. Baines, *Education Best Promoted By Perfect Freedom* (1854), 28–9, 30, 32–3, 44–5

I   The secular alternative

It is a satisfactory feature of the argumentation and criticism, and even of the abuse called forth by the Conference, that they involve a clear recognition of the position which the Nonconformists at Manchester have assumed in regard to State-aided Schools. There was indeed little room for misapprehension. No company of men ever came together who more thoroughly knew their own minds, or who gave to their common conviction a more simple and intelligible expression. The trumpet gave no uncertain sound. The Conference unanimously and unfalteringly took its stand on what has been called, not very happily, 'the secular platform'. . . .

There were few even among Dissenters who were prepared for the enthusiasm and unanimity with which the Conference adopted its resolution. It had been boldly said by men who professed to know that there was no party among Nonconformists prepared to accept a system of national education which excluded religion from its subjects of teaching, but only here and there a noisy individual, whose political prejudices had blunted his religious sensibilities. Their testimony had the usual good fortune of hardy and unqualified assertions often repeated; it was so far believed by many whose own observation would have led them to a contrary conclusion, that they doubted whether a general conference would not bring out such an irreconcilable antagonism of view among Nonconformists as would disable them for further action in the education controversy. The tone and decision of the Conference were a grateful surprise to those who had been thus misled; though it is difficult to imagine anyone who knew the inner history or even only the historical antecedents of Nonconformity, supposing that when the religious question involved in a national system of education came to be closely grappled with, Nonconformists could take any other position than that to which they committed themselves at Manchester. . . .

If the ground taken by Nonconformists at Manchester in regard to State-aided schools be not sound, and in the spirit of a true political philosophy, then the whole basis of Nonconformity is unsound. For the resolutions of the Conference in favour of a strictly secular system were but an application to schools of the principles which Nonconformists seek to apply to churches. There are individual Nonconformists it is true, who dissent from the Church of England, mainly, if not exclusively, on doctrinal grounds. They would explain their position by the phrase 'Evangelical Nonconformity'. But outside the pale of Conference Wesleyanism, they form no considerable party among Dissenters. Modern English Nonconformity not merely dissents from the English Church, but repudiates the State-Church principle. This is not the place fully to expound, much less to defend their theory of the Church. . . .

It is not that they hold the Church to be clean and the State unclean, the Church holy and the State unholy. They regard a well-ordered and righteous civil government as not less a divine institution than the Church. But the civil government they hold to be charged with the care of man's temporal interests and to have no kind of equipment for other service; while the Church is endued with spiritual energy, and inhabited by the Divine Regenerator, that it may help men in all that concerns the conquest of sin.

Throughout the education controversy, Nonconformists, looking to their distinctive principles, have had a choice of consistent positions. It was open to them to demand that the State should leave the education of the people to voluntary agency; and this they were bound to do if they included religious teaching in their idea of education. Or it was open to them to invite the State to take part in the education of the people; but in that event they were bound by their distinctive principles to require that in doing so it should limit itself to secular teaching. And to this alternative their choice was limited. It has taken some time to make the ground clear, but the Manchester Conference showed that it is made clear at last. And now it can hardly be said that there is a choice. The nation has irrevocably determined that it will hold the government bound to see to it, that every English child receives the elements of a sound education. If the whole body of Nonconformists were to take the ground which the majority are supposed to have taken twenty-five years ago, it would not avail. The die is cast in favour of a State-aided system of public schools. A few may sullenly maintain the

old ground of Voluntaryism, but they will exercise no influence on
the course of events. The only course left open for Nonconformists,
therefore, is to demand, and reiterate their demand, and not to rest
satisfied until they prevail, that the State confine its educational action
to the teaching of secular subjects; . . . while it is natural for the
advocates of a State Church to insist on the competence of the State
to teach religion in the public schools, Nonconformists cannot give
their consent without disloyalty to Nonconformist principles.

The argument for a rigidly secular system drawn from the unfitness of
the methods of public law to further the ends of religion, will be conclusive to the great majority of Nonconformists.

> The Conference of Nonconformists at Man-
> chester, as reported in the *British Quarterly
> Review*, Volume 55 (1872), 507, 509, 521,
> 522-3

J   The Bible and the Board Schools

A Meeting of Nonconformists was held on Monday evening in St
James' Hall, Mr McArthur M.P., in the chair, in opposition to sectarian
teaching at the cost of the State. . . .

The Reverend J. G. Rogers moved: 'That in relation to schools
established or aided by local school boards out of the rates, this meeting
believes that the difficulties of the case may be met by prohibiting the
use therein of any religious catechisms or formularies, or the teaching
of anything in opposition to, or in support of, the tenets of any sect—
this prohibition not to apply to the use of the Holy Scriptures, but
such use, wherever adopted, to be under the regulation of the time table
conscience-clause, so that the attendance of any child at such Bible
lessons shall not be compulsory.'

The Reverend C. H. Spurgeon seconded the motion. Nevertheless he
did not sympathize with much of what he had heard. He trusted he
should never allow his Nonconformity to outride his Christianity or
love for the Bible. He was sorry to differ from what he felt the current
of the meeting, but his opinion was that Government had better have
left education alone—(cheers, and 'No, no'). If the Nonconformists of
England had been logical, they would, instead of allowing the Government to touch it, have been more liberal themselves in its support.
It was a gross falsehood to say that Voluntaryism had failed. The

Nonconformists now had made a great concession, but they had
violated their logical position. His conscience required that the Bible
should be read in the school where the children were taught, and if the
Bible were excluded, he would preach defiance of the government up
and down the land. He believed the majority of Nonconformists
agreed with him—(cheers, and 'No, no').

The motion having been carried, the meeting separated.

Report in the *Inquirer*, 18 June 1870

K   Popular education: a Wesleyan view

The Methodist people have made great sacrifices in order to secure
efficient Methodist teachers, and surely they have a right to expect that
they will be produced. Their expectations may be unreasonable in
some other respects, but they ought not to be disappointed in this. . . .

Professor Huxley says that our educational ladder should have its
foot in the gutter and its top in the university. We . . . say that our ladder should have its foot in the home, and its top in heaven. That the
children should be cared for by Christian parents in infancy, should
enter the school, pass through it into the church militant, and so on to
the Church triumphant. . . .

Wherever you go, be sure to reverence the children committed to
your care. They will often be wild and unlovable, and familiarity will
tempt you to underestimate them; but guard against this. Remember
they are all God's children made by Him, redeemed by Him, loved by
Him, and that He Who said, 'Honour all men' is especially saying,
'Honour the children'. They are of priceless value.

> The sun is but a spark of fire,
> A transient meteor in the sky;
> The child, immortal as its Sire,
> Can never die.

They must live for ever, either amidst the saved in heaven, or the
lost in hell, and which it shall be will greatly depend on you. 'Take heed
therefore, that you despise not one of these little ones'. . . .

You and your children must meet again at the great tribunal. Then
there will be a review of your work, and as you stand amid the scholars
you have won for Christ, you will say with holy joy, 'Here am I, and
the children Thou gavest me.' And He will say, 'Well done, thou good

and faithful servant; thou hast been faithful over a few things, I will
make thee ruler over many things: enter thou into the joy of thy Lord.'

C. Garrett: *Loving Counsels* (1887), 226, 228,
230, 302. From an address to the students of
the Westminster and Southlands College

L   The onslaught on the municipalities

It will be necessary that important improvements should be made in
our present system for promoting popular education. You beyond all
other classes in the community, are interested in these improvements
being made promptly and energetically. . . . I therefore believe that
while the present system should be left unimpaired, powers should
be granted to municipal bodies, and to parishes or counties, to found
new schools, to be sustained partly by rates and partly by grants from
the imperial revenue. And if in poor and neglected districts local
authorities should refuse to exercise those powers, I would have the
duty enforced by the central government. Any scheme that would
transfer the whole conduct of popular education to a government
office in London I would regard with grave apprehension; but it is
possible to unite local management with central superintendence and
inspection. . . .

I earnestly hope that before long . . . there will be working men
sitting on the sacred benches at Westminster. But you cannot help
seeing that there are very serious difficulties in the way before this can
be accomplished. I want to remind you that it is not within the walls of
the House of Commons merely that you may develop and explain
your political principles. Convert the constituencies, and you convert
the House.

Send up and down the country men who shall be able to defend,
illustrate and enforce the measures which appear to you to be necessary
for the removal of grave abuses. . . . If you find that you cannot as yet
send men of your own class to the House, send them to the lecture rooms
and public halls of every town in the country, from Berwick to Ply-
mouth, and you will do more to control the course of legislation than
by sending a few working men to Parliament. Let clubs be formed. . . .
And if I might be permitted to repeat in public what I have already
privately suggested to some of the members of the Council of the
Birmingham Branch of the Reform League, I should strongly advise
that the branches of the League throughout the country prepare to
assume a new form . . . in order that you may establish political

institutes in every borough for promoting lectures and public meetings to diffuse a knowledge of liberal principles in relation to all national affairs, and to maintain the union and intensify the earnestness of all sections of the liberal party. . . .

I cannot see why our great towns might not be made more tolerable places to live in; why the filth in which some wretched people are satisfied to exist and which originates many forms of disease from which their neighbours suffer as well as themselves, should not be more resolutely punished, and indeed rendered almost impossible; why the provisions which secure free air and cleanliness in some factories and workshops should not be extended to trades which are as yet altogether uncontrolled; why there should not be several open spaces reserved in every great town for children to play in; why new districts lying outside the boundaries of our boroughs should not be compelled to keep their streets cleaner and get better drainage . . . it will be the fault of the new electors if they do not insist on such improvements as these. . . .

It is not those who occupy the highest social position, but those who occupy the lowest, whose power we have to restrain and from whose tyranny we have to emancipate ourselves.

Take the Borough of Birmingham alone. We have no frowning castle overlooking and threatening the town, the stronghold of a feudal baron and filled with armed men, permitted by their lord to rob and illtreat men at their pleasure. But we have what is perhaps worse than this. We have a vast gaol which is far more costly to support than were any of the strongholds of the robber chiefs that once dwelt in the castles of the Rhine. . . .

You have a great practical concern in whatever measures are likely to make the criminal classes disappear, and I trust that such measures will have your hearty support. . . .

There is another class from which we have almost as much to fear . . . one million persons receiving relief. . . . And in this million you have first the permanent paupers, and then a vast mass of people who are on the parish on and off again every few months, but who when they go off are sure to leave successors. . . . We have hereditary paupers, as well as hereditary criminals, and I maintain that this is intolerable. . . . You will feel very distinctly the sharp pressure that comes upon the community for the support of the 'armies of the homeless and unfed', and will be the more eager to discover how the pauperism of the country can be effectively diminished.

R. W. Dale, The Politics of the Future, A Lecture to the New Electors (1867), 7–11, 14–17

M   'A more generous recognition of the claims of the masses'

Briefly my view is that the Liberal Party has been utterly demoralized by Forster and Gladstone; that, in this state, an attack of Tories and Publicans combined was, and might have been expected to be, irresistible.

The only chance of the Government lay in a declaration of policy calculated to arouse the hearty enthusiasm of the non-conformists and the working-classes. Instead of this Gladstone issued the meanest manifesto that ever proceeded from a great Minister.

On the whole the radical party will gain by finding themselves face to face with avowed foes, instead of having to wrestle with pretended friends. At the same time, the returns show that the present political position of the Dissenters is not satisfactory.

They are very hazy as to principles in the Education question, and have been, in many cases, carried over to the enemy by the 'Bible' cry. Worse still, they have ceased to combine cordially with the working classes, without whose active assistance further advances in the direction of Religious Equality are impossible. But both in the case of the agricultural labourers, and in reference to the demands of the Trades Unions for the repeal of what I do not hesitate to stigmatize as class legislation of the worst kind, the Dissenters have largely held aloof, and their organs in the Press, the 'Daily News' for instance, have been unsympathetic and even hostile.

Unless this is altered in the future such questions as Disestablishment and Disendowment will be indefinitely postponed, as the Artisan voter can see little difference between Caesar and Pompey, and looking at the whole affair as a mere squabble between Church and Chapel, will take no interest in the matter.

The only districts in which Liberalism has come well out of the recent fight are the Midland Counties, where we have gained on the whole one seat, and the Northern Counties, where the balance is still more in our favour. In both these cases the local leader has appealed directly to the mass of the working-class population—the Dissenters aiding very largely with their purses and influence, and cordially recognizing the justice of the labourers' claims in the two questions I have named.

Both these districts have been well-served by a really Liberal Press— the 'Daily Post' and 'Morning News' in Birmingham, and the 'News

Chronicle' in Newcastle-on-Tyne having been persistently educating the people for years past.

I feel that this narrowness on the part of many of the rank and file of Dissent, will be fatal to the success of our special aims, unless we can induce and make a more generous recognition of the claims of the masses.

I write this much because I hope the influence of your Review may be used to further a closer union between nonconformists as such and the working classes.

J. Chamberlain to Henry Allon, 13 February 1874 in A Peel (ed.), *Letters to a Victorian Editor* (1929)

6

NONCONFORMITY
AND THE WORLD

The history of nineteenth-century Dissent is intrinsically bound up with the history of Revival of which the traditional English variety, the Wesleyan, deeply experienced but restrained, needs to be distinguished from what may be called the sub-Wesleyan, with its groanings, rolling and other physical accompaniments (**A**). When, at the end of the 1830s these spontaneous forms were on the wane, visiting American preachers, of whom Caughey and Finney were the most celebrated, revived the tradition with new American emphases upon organizing the congregation so as to exploit the maximum emotional impact. In 1859, came a reawakening, which though running parallel to developments in America also had its own indigenous origins. Together with the campaigns of Moody and Sankey in the seventies and after, they made a powerful impact upon Dissent. Moody, though imitating earlier American visitors in his emphasis upon organization was mercifully free from cant. He secured widespread approval from all Dissenters, except Unitarians at one end and hyper-Calvinists at the other; witness R. W. Dale's attack upon Archbishop Tait's withholding of official sanction from the evangelist (**B**(i)–(iii)).

The revival meeting was not the only approach to the multitude: from the 1840s no city church was complete without one, two, or in some cases as many as a dozen branch missions in those poorer areas, where there lived England's own heathen, together with those immigrants who brought the mission-field to the heart of the capital itself. Browning's experience of one of these in 'Christmas Eve' might be immediately repulsive, though later in the poem he came to a rather more generous estimation of its function (**C**). Very often, however, the mission hall was not merely a religious institution but a kind of relief or social service centre, with its clothing societies, penny banks and tontine clubs, soup kitchens and other agencies (**D**). In like fashion, the colporteur, here exemplified from the journal of Thomas Alcorn, was also evangelist and social worker (**E**).

The considerable Nonconformist investment of men, money and energy in overseas missions (**F**) is all too easily misunderstood: for example the popular notion that the Nonconformist conscience was more sensitive abroad than at home probably owes more to Dickens's Mrs Jellyby (whose dress and home and family perpetuated disorder whilst she devoted herself to the needs of the inhabitants of Borrioboola Gha) than to any more scholarly judgment. The evangelistic motive, the desire to save 'multitudes of heathen perishing ever-lastingly', the dominant inspiration of the early part of the period (G) had, as the century progressed, except amongst conservative evangelicals such as Hudson Taylor, the founder of the China Inland Mission, to compete with other forms of motivation. Similarly the missionary impact could not narrowly be confined to religious issues: the collision between Nonconformist polity and the mores and traditional social structures overseas was inevitably, in some cases, violent (H). It was in vain that the Missionary Societies at home, where 'the missionary is not popular at the Foreign Office', strove to confine him strictly to his religious duties: the more sturdily democratic his denominational position, the more readily would the missionary reject the restraints of missionary bureaucrats and identify himself with the social and political aspirations of his adopted people (I). And yet whilst Dissenters in the very nature of the case were intrinsically suspicious of Empire, they could not altogether escape the jingoism of the 1890s, especially when refined as 'social imperialism'—it was within such terms that the missionary apologia was rephrased at the end of the century (J and K).

Professor Ward has taught us that denominationalism was a child of the 1810s and 20s and that it contrasts strangely with the undenominational Protestantism of the beginning of the nineteenth century:[1] this new creation was least appropriate on the mission-field which continued to pose the advantages of Christian co-operation if not of church unity (L). Reinforced by fears of Rome and infidelity, this same missionary concern was a principal ingredient of the Evangelical Alliance which re-created in 1846 amongst both Church and Chapel Evangelicals something of the undenominational protestantism of the previous century, though not without soul-searching debate (M(i) and (ii)). Within the recognized groupings of Dissent some measures of reunion were witnessed in the century (the United Methodist Free Churches of 1856, Presbyterian Union in 1876, the Particular and New Connexion General Baptists in 1891). This led on to the movement for Free Church unity which looked unsuccessfully for some larger measure of organizational amalgamation: it began with a frank desire to heal past breaches for the presentation of a more effective witness, but in a decade when Nonconformity was more open to self-analysis than ever before, the underlying social pressures are more marked and more readily acknowledged. That these could be interpreted in totally different ways is shown by the aggressive, hectoring tone of Hugh Price Hughes, the Wesleyan leader who did more than any other man to align his communion with the rest of the Free Churches (N(i)) and the timorous apologetic of the Congregationalist, R. F. Horton (N(ii)).

[1] W. R. Ward, 'Popular Religion and the Problem of Control' in *Studies in Church History*, Volume 8 (1972), 237–57, and 'The Last Chronicle of Barset', in *The Journal of Ecclesiastical History'* xviii (1967), 65–70.

A   Enthusiasm scorned?

'Then, sir, if you're curious about such things, you had better go a little higher up the hill, and hear the people at Mr Aitken's chapel: they're still going on; and you'll say, sir, you never heard or saw such things in your life!'

'Indeed! what do they call themselves?'

'They aren't the regular Methodists—they're a bad sort of Methodists—Jumpers or Ranters, or something of that sort. They're a most horrid nuisance, sir, in the neighbourhood, and I wish the law would put them down.' . . .

I encountered a scene which I will attempt with faithful exactitude to describe. It was a large, low room, lit with gas, and there were several groups of people in it, men and women—some singing, some praying—others groaning and writhing on the floor—some standing, others kneeling, others sitting. Some were really *shrieking* in the wildest and maddest way imaginable! The group nearest me consisted of some twenty or thirty, surrounding about half a dozen people who were on their knees, with whom most of them were praying, uttering horrid groans and ejaculations—sometimes wringing and other times clapping their hands. They were 'assisting souls in the agonies of the new birth', as they termed it; that is, persons who were seeking to be converted. I went nearer, and beheld a decently-dressed middle-aged woman kneeling beside one of the would-be neophytes—a young man—tossing herself about in all directions, lifting up and down her arms in a frantic manner, and violently striking the form before which she knelt, at one time praying, at another shouting into his ear—'Believe, believe, man, believe—oh, come to Jesus, come to Him—don't wait! Don't delay a moment! Doesn't thee see Him? Here He is—He is in the midst of us—He's waiting for thee! Take him by the hand, blessed Lord! Oh, Lord Jesus, o dear Lord, Thou must save this lad! Come along lad, He's waiting for thee! Oh, Jesus, why do thy chariot-wheels delay? Pluck him like a brand from the burning.'

'O-o-o-oh, Lord Jesus!' heavily groaned the subject of her praying.

'Why don't you believe? Why don't you believe?' she exclaimed, vehemently, literally slapping him on the back; who, his face hid in his arms, his body sprawling and writhing about the floor and against the form, seemed to make direful efforts to second those of her beside him sighing and groaning in a most dismal manner. . . .

'Ay, pray thus, and He *must* come; He can't help himself; He loves it! Come! thou must believe now! The devil will have thee this night if

thou doesn't!—there—that's it—that's it!' as the wretched fellow
redoubled his groans and contortions—'Wrestle, wrestle! Jesus loves a
good *wrestler*; he loves to be beat; He'll love thee all the better for this
good fight. Don't ye see Him? Pray, man; *now's* the time! Now's the
accepted time, now's the day of salvation—now, now or never! Don't
thee feel it, thinkest thou?' The man, I suppose, answered in the
affirmative, for the woman on the other side, in a still wilder manner,
suddenly shouted, 'O, Thank Thee, Jesus! Thank Thee! Thank Thee!
I knew Thou wouldn't be long; Glory! Glory!. . . .'

'Who is the minister of this place?' I enquired, as drily and frigidly as
possible, thinking thus to parry their attack.

'Mr Aitken, sir', replied the last-mentioned man.

'What is the name of the body of Christians who worship here?' I
continued with a very polite but distant air.

'This is the Church of Christ—the mystical body of Christ; we are
his people, and He is here. He's waiting to save you' said the first
man. . . .

I quitted the room, to get rid of his pestilent importunities, with
feelings of mingled pity, indignation, astonishment, contempt.

Anon, 'My First Circuit: Law and Facts from
the North' in Blackwood's Magazine, Volume
44 (1838), 88–91

B   Mr Moody and Mr Sankey

(i)   *The Rally*

Mr Bright spoke in the Hall that night, and it was most inconveniently
crowded: but some of the police were of opinion that on several of the
following evenings the crowd that filled the Hall for the religious
services was denser than that which filled it for the political demonstration. Night after night, long before the hour of service, long rows
of carriages stood in the street, filled with persons who hoped that
when the crowd about the doors had thinned, they might be able to
find standing room inside, and thousands streamed away because they
found they had come too late to have a chance of pressing in. . . .

How is all this to be accounted for?

'You advertised the Americans well', it has been said, 'by holding
special prayer-meetings every day for three weeks before they came—
prayer-meetings in which all the Evangelical Nonconformists and

some of the Evangelical clergy united.' Well, no doubt the prayer-meetings were a kind of 'advertisement' of the services and assisted to attract large numbers on the first few days.

It is said again: 'The local newspapers helped you.' One of them published a series of articles on Mr Moody and Mr Sankey before they came, describing the impression they had produced in Scotland and Ireland. The *Morning News* generally gave several columns day after day to reports of the services; the *Daily Post* . . . . gave great prominence to them: and even the local Conservative organ, the *Daily Gazette*, always had enough about 'Messrs. Moody and Sankey' to attract attention. . . .

It is also true that the local committee advertised the services most efficiently. The walls of the town were covered with their placards, and these were constantly renewed. . . .

Some people have said that it is easy to get crowds of women to 'hysterical' religious services. But although the morning and afternoon meetings were largely attended by women, I believe that the majority of the evening congregation always consisted of men, and of men of all kinds—rough lads of seventeen or eighteen, workingmen, clerks, tradesmen and manufacturers. . . .

Nor were the services at all 'hysterical'; the first sign of hysterical excitement was instantly repressed by Mr Moody, and although I attended a very large number of the meetings, I saw nothing of the kind again. It was very curious too, that although the crowds were so enormous, very few women fainted. I do not remember more than three or four cases. . . .

How, I ask again, is the great interest of the people in these services to be accounted for? The truest, simplest, and most complete reply to the question which I can give is that the power of God was manifested in an extraordinary degree in connection with them; but there were concurrent circumstances which deserve notice. . . .

I attribute very much to a fact which is perhaps not sufficiently recognized by any of us. There is, I believe, a very large number of persons—many of them regularly attending public worship, many of them never crossing the threshold of church or chapel—who have had deep religious impressions, which have not issued in a clear decision to serve Christ, but which have left a dull aching of heart for God. . . . When such people heard that within a very few months thousands of men and women had declared that, while listening to Mr Moody and Mr Sankey, they had passed from religious indifference or despondency into the clear light of God, they began to think that for them too there might be hope. I think it probable that many of the 'converts' will be found to have belonged to this forgotten class. . . .

Mr Sankey's solos evidently touched very many hearts; and the effect produced by the manner in which the vast audiences united in such songs as 'Hold the fort, for I am coming', 'Safe in the arms of Jesus' and 'The great Physician now is near', was sometimes very thrilling. The 'songs' have been sharply criticized. It is very easy to criticize them; it might be more profitable to consider why it is that both the music and the words are so popular and effective. . . . Mr Sankey's melodies—whatever their demerits—are caught by thousands of people of all kinds, cultivated and uncultivated, men, women, and children, and are sung with a will. . . .

The same principles are applicable to the hymns. Critics have said that they are 'childish', that they have no 'literary merit', that there is something ridiculous in hearing a congregation of grown people sing- ing with enthusiasm, 'I am so glad that Jesus loves me'. Well, the fact that hymns which are simple even to childishness are sung by grown people with so much earnestness, that hymns with no 'literary merit' kindle new fire in the hearts of men and women who know something of Shakespeare, Milton and Wordsworth is surely worth investigating. Is it the 'childishness' which accounts for their power? Is it the absence of 'literary merit'? I think not. Give the people a collection of hymns characterized by equal fervour, expressing with the same directness the elementary convictions and the deepest emotions of the Christian heart . . . and they will become equally popular and more enduring. But our hymn books are too stiff and cold. People want to sing, not what they *think* but what they *feel*. . . .

One of the elements of Mr Moody's power consists in his perfect naturalness. He has something to say, and he says it—says it as simply and directly to thirteen thousand people as to thirteen. He has nothing of the impudence into which some speakers are betrayed when they try to be easy and unconventional; but he talks in a perfectly unrestrained and straightforward way, just as he would talk to half a dozen friends at his fireside. . . .

It is objected that he is too 'familiar' with sacred things. Generally— not always—the objection comes from persons who are extremely *unfamiliar* with them. . . . Mr Moody is, no doubt, very 'familiar' with things about which he talks. He is like a man who keeps Sunday every day in the week; his mind does not put on Sunday clothes when he begins to talk about religion. . . .

Some people say that he is 'irreverant'. If he is, I must have been singularly fortunate, for I have never heard him say anything which justifies the charge. But what people seem to mean is that he does not regard with religious respect everyone that is mentioned in the Bible. Why should he? When he said that Bartimaeus, after getting his sight, was eager to go home and 'see what kind of a looking woman he had for a wife, for you know that as yet he had never seen Mrs Bartimaeus', some people who saw the report in the newspapers thought this was a proof of the irreverance of which he is said to be guilty. As a matter of taste most of us would prefer to describe the woman as the 'wife' of the blind man; but why the 'Mrs' should be thought irreverent is difficult to understand. Reverence is due to God alone, and to our Lord Jesus. . . .

(ii)   The After-meeting

The galleries were a beautiful sight. . . . Cultivated young ladies were sitting or standing with girls of their own age, sometimes with two or three together, whose eager faces indicated the earnestness of their desire to understand how they were to lay hold of the great blessing. Young men were talking to lads—some of their own social position, others with black hands and rough clothes, which were suggestive of gun-making and rolling-mills and brass foundries. Ladies of refinement were trying to make the truth clear to women whose worn faces and poor dress told of the hardships of their daily life. Men of business, local politicians, were at the same work with men of forty or fifty years of age. And there was the brightness of hope and faith in the tone and manner and hearing of nearly all of them. . . .

(iii)   Reply to the Archbishop of Canterbury

I have lived all my life among tradesmen, manufacturers and working people. Only now and then, by accident, have I any opportunity of learning for myself the ways of thinking and the habits of life which are common in rich and fashionable society. I believe that there are large numbers of devout and excellent people in the upper classes, as there are in the lower classes. But nothing that I have ever heard leads me to think that there are clearer signs of the millenium in the West End of London than in the East. The neighbourhood of the Opera House in the Haymarket where Mr Moody has been preaching is no more like a suburb of the New Jerusalem than the neighbourhood of Whitechapel Church.

If I may put any confidence in what I have heard repeatedly from

intelligent and cultivated men, who live among wealthy and aristocratic people, there is a wide-spread and growing unbelief among the
higher classes of English society which resists all the efforts of the clergy
to subdue it. It is not likely to be subdued by the most scholarly arguments, by books on the evidences of the Christian religion, by replies
to Mr Mill's essays, and to Dr Tyndall's doctrine of prayer. The history
of religious thought in England during the last century is familiar to
the Archbishop of Canterbury. He knows that this country was rescued
from atheism—not by scholarly and dignified Boyle lecturers. . . . but
by the faith and zeal of evangelists who did their work without the
'official sanction' of the clergy, without the 'direct sanction' of the
bishops, and in the teeth of the hostility of the 'respectable classes' of
English society. I believe that the scepticism and irreligion of our own
times—among the rich as well as among the poor—must also be overcome not by logic and learning, though these too have their appropriate and appointed functions—but by such manifestations of the
power of God as we in Birmingham have seen in connection with
Mr Moody's services. When men cease to believe that a sun ever shone
in the heavens, the glory of a sunrise is the true remedy for their
unbelief.

> R.W. Dale, *Mr. Moody and Mr. Sankey* (1875),
> 7, 8–10, 13–15, 18–19, 21; *The Day of Salva-
> tion, A Reply to The Letter of the Archbishop of
> Canterbury* (1875), 24–5

C   'Where earthly aids being cast behind, His All in All appears serene'

> Well, from the road, the lanes or the common,
> In came the flock: the fat, weary woman,
> Panting and bewildered, down-clapping
> Her umbrella with a mighty report,
> Grounded it by me, wry and flapping,
> A wreck of whalebones; then, with a snort,
> Like a startled horse, at the interloper,
> (Who humbly knew himself improper,
> But could not shrink up small enough)
> —Round to the door, and in—the gruff
> Hinge's invariable scold
> Making my very blood run cold.

Prompt in the wake of her, up-pattered
On broken clogs, the many-tattered
Little old-faced peaking sister-turned-mother
Of the sickly babe she tried to smother
Somehow up, with its spotted face,
From the cold, on her breast, the one warm place;
She too must stoop, wring the poor ends dry
Of a draggled shawl, and add thereby
Her tribute to the door-mat, sopping
Already from my own clothes dripping,
Which yet she seemed to grudge I should stand on. . . .
Close on her heels the dingy satins
Of a female something past me flitted,
With lips as much too white, as a streak
Lay far too red on each hollow cheek;
And it seemed the very door-hinge pitied
All that was left of a woman once,
Holding at least its tongue for the nonce.
Then a tall, yellow man, like the Penitent Thief,
With his jaw bound up in a handkerchief,
And eyelids screwed together tight,
Led himself in by some inner light. . . .
Accordingly, as a shoemaker's lad,
With wizened face in want of soap,
And wet apron round his waist like a rope,
(After stopping outside, for his cough was bad,
To get the fit over, poor gentle creature,
And so avoid disturbing the preacher)
—Passed in, I sent my elbow spikewise
At the shutting door, and entered likewise,
Received the hinge's accustomed greeting.
And crossed the threshold's magic pentacle,
And found myself in full conventicle,
To wit, in Zion Chapel Meeting,
On the Christmas-eve of 'Forty-nine,
Which, calling its flock to their special clover,
Found all assembled, and one sheep over,
Whose lot, as the weather pleased, was mine.

I very soon had enough of it.
The hot smell and the human noises,

And my neighbour's coat, the greasy cuff of it,
Were a pebble stone that a child's hand poises,
Compared with the pig-of-lead-like pressure
Of the preaching man's immense stupidity,
As he poured his doctrine forth, full measure,
To melt his audience's avidity.
You needed not the wit of a Sybil,
To guess the cause of it all, in a twinkling;
No sooner our friend had got an inkling
Of treasure hid in the Holy Bible. . . .
Then he handled it so, in fine irreverence,
As to hug the Book of Books to pieces;
And, a patchwork of chapters and texts in severance. . . .
—So he tossed you again your Holy Scriptures. . . .
But the flock sat on, divinely flustered,
Sniffing, methought, its dew of Hermon,
With such content in every snuffle,
As the devil inside us loves to ruffle.
My fat old woman purred with pleasure,
And, thumb round thumb, went twirling faster,
While she, to his periods keeping measure,
Maternally devoured the pastor.
The man with the handkerchief untied it,
Showed us a horrible wen inside it,
Gave his eyelids yet another screwing,
And rocked himself as the woman was doing.
The shoemaker's lad, discreetly choking,
Kept down his cough. 'Twas too provoking!
My gorge rose at the nonsense and stuff of it;
So, saying like Eve, when she plucked the apple,
'I wanted a taste, and now there's enough of it',
I flung out of the little chapel.

Robert Browning, *Christmas Eve* (1850)

D City missions

(i) *The Irish of London*

A more important field than is presented by the Irish in London for missionary effort, it is difficult to conceive. So far as numbers are concerned, they present a larger claim than many of the entire stations of our Foreign Missionary Societies. The Irish in London, of the poorer classes alone, amount to 200,000. But the entire (sic) of the 'Colony of the Cape of Good Hope' in 1848, was no more, and of the natives there were but 123,719. New Zealand is computed at but from 120,000 to 180,000, and the entire colony of Sierra Leone in 1838 was only 41,551, or scarcely more than one-fifth of the population of the poor Irish of London; while Greenland, that field of successful missionary enterprise by the Moravians is less than a twentieth part of the number. Is it then consistent to send missionaries to those afar off, at a necessarily great cost, and to pass by those who are dwelling in the midst of our own metropolis? The one ought to be done, but the other ought still more not to be left undone. As 500 families, consisting of about 2,000 individuals, are as many as one lay visitor can take charge of with any advantage, there are actually *one hundred* such faithful men wanted for the Irish alone of London.

(ii)   Ragged Schools

The 'Devil's Acre', as it is familiarly known in the neighbourhood, is the square block comprised between Dean, Peter and Tothill-streets, and Strutton-ground. It is permeated by Orchard-street, St Anne's-street, Old and New Pye-streets, Pear-street, Perkins'-rents and Duck-lane. From some of these, narrow covered passage-ways lead into small quadrangular courts, containing but a few crazy, tumble-down-looking houses, and inhabited by characters of the most equivocal description. The district which is small in area, is one of the most populous in London, almost every house being crowded with numerous families and multitudes of lodgers. There are other parts of the town as filthy, dingy, and forbidding in appearance as this, but these are generally the haunts more of poverty than crime. But there are none in which guilt of all kinds and degrees converges in such volume as on this, the moral plague-spot, not only of the metropolis, but also of the kingdom. And yet from almost every point of it you can observe the towers of the Abbey peering down upon you, as if they were curious to observe that to which they seem to be indifferent.

Such is the spot which true Christian benevolence has, for some time, marked as a chosen field for its most unostentatious operations. It was first taken possession of, with a view to its improvement, by the London City Mission, a body represented in the district by a single missionary, who has now been for about 12 years labouring—and not without success—in the arduous work of its purification; and who, by his

energy, tact and perseverance, has acquired such an influence over its
turbulent and lawless population, as makes him a safer escort to the
stranger desirous of visiting it, than a whole posse of police. By the aid
of several opulent philanthropists whom he has interested in his labours
he has reared up within the district two schools, which are numerously
attended by the squalid children of the neighbourhood—one of these
schools having an Industrial Department connected with it. An exclusively Industrial School for boys of more advanced age has also been
established, which has recently been attached to the Ragged School
Union.

> J. Garwood, *The Million Peopled City; or One
> Half of the People of London made known to
> the Other Half* (1853), 278, and C. Dickens
> *Household Words* cited by J. Garwood *ibid.*,
> 37–8

E   The colporteur

Tuesday 23rd March 1852. Visited 15 families in Courts off Richmond
Row and Cuerdon Street; distributed 15 tracts, read portions of the
Word, made remarks upon them, and in my conversation with the
people generally, I endeavoured to teach them Man's guilt as a fallen
sinner, and the only way of having guilt removed, by the blood of the
Cross. I had a conversation with several R.C.'s today, they all refused
to receive tracts, but I would not give up, without leaving a testimony
behind me. One said, she would hear nothing but what related to love
or murder. I told her that was the story I wished chiefly to tell, and that
both met in the Cross of Jesus. He was murdered by wicked hands, he
was crucified and slain, yet in his sufferings and death, We have the
manifestation of the love of God to perishing, damnation-deserving
sinners: and declared in her hearing the absolute certainty of eternal life
to all who come to God, through the finished work of Jesus, and the
absolute impossibility of getting to Heaven or enjoying eternal life in
any other way.

Thursday 25th April 1853 ... Addressed the females in the Peniten-
tiary N. Road at 8 o'clock from the first clause of the ninth verse of the
thirteenth of Mark: 'But take heed to yourselves'. Referred (sic) to the
very melancholy accident which had so very recently occurred at the
place, by one of the inmates falling into an old, dry well about 160
feet in depth, as an appeal to them to take heed to themselves lest they

fall into that dismal pit in which there is no water and out of which there is none to deliver: pointing them to the Lord Jesus as the only almighty deliverer from the Wrath to come, and the Saviour of all who come to Him.

Monday 2nd June 1856. Visited 14 families in Harding Street enforcing the duty of turning to the Lord from the various dumb idols. Had a pretty lengthy conversation with an R.C. Tried to be faithful without giving offence, but the truth pierces even when the heart continues blind and hard. It is ours to testify of Jesus, whether the testimony be received or not. I have often had to blame myself for anticipating consequences. I was not long sitting in a house when the Master, as he is generally called, introduced the trial of Palmer, saying he had never heard anything like it before. I told him that I had read of a more wonderful trial, that though the witnesses were known to be false, though the Judge declared he could find no fault in the Prisoner, yet the general cry was that he was guilty of death, and so he was put to death. The man asked if that had happened in this Country: He was greatly amazed, denouncing the injustice. I told him that I thought he had read this trial himself, but he could not recollect until I mentioned Jesus before Pilate. He seemed affected, when I pressed the Cause of his Sufferings and Death, and that his enemies to this day, the ungodly, are no better affected towards Him than then. Addressed the needlewomen at 7 o'clock from part of the 13th Luke.

> Extracts from the Mss. *Journal of Thomas Alcorn, Agent of the Liverpool Town Mission, 1851–1857*, in the possession of Dr Ian Sellers

F Missionary investments

'To what purpose is this waste?' This very question confronts us today in presence of the missionary enterprise. Reckon up the outlay; valuable time given to it by men to whom time is gold—valuable time, and much thought and energy; a large amount of money contributed every year; not large, perhaps, when set over against what we are able to give, or what we spend on luxury and pride, yet very considerable, and annually increasing; and, lastly, a large expenditure of human life. In the beginning of our mission in India, sickness followed sickness, and man after man fell; and in our youngest mission—that on the Congo—it has been the same, only more deadly; indeed, to some onlookers, the

going of our missionaries thither seems like that ride into the jaws of
death at Balaclava. Every man who goes out goes at the peril of his life;
and we have no security, as yet, that the risk is materially abated. . . .

It is clear, that we are bound to place a high and sacred value on the
lives of our missionaries; to pray for them, to use all the measures that
science and experience suggest for their safety, and to man our stations
sufficiently, so that no life may be endangered through the overstrain of
care and labour in an unfavourable climate. Precious in the sight of the
Lord is the death of His saints; and precious should it be in our sight
also.

All this being not simply admitted, freely and without burden, but
insisted on, we can survey the mission field at large, or any part of it,
and can face the question squarely. To what purpose is this waste—this
expenditure of treasure and of life?

The first thing to take into account is, that we are acting under
Christ's Commission, which requires us to carry the message of salvation to the whole world. As widely as the curse of sin extends, so
widely must the tidings of mercy reach. This is not debatable matter,
and therefore need not be dwelt upon. To argue it in such an assembly
as this were a piece of foolish impertinence. It is settled among us, once
for all. By the will of Jesus Christ, this round earth, in all its isles and
continents, must hear the great evangel of heaven. Africa cannot be
missed out. It has been put upon us in providential ways to undertake
service of the most important kind in that continent. . . .

'The blood of the martyr', they said in the old days, 'is the seed of the
Church;' and the principle of the words is as true and as applicable
today as ever. . . .

Many in the missionary band I do not hesitate to call 'martyrs',
ranking them with those who have gone to the stake or the scaffold for
the truth's sake, and who by their death have helped to pay the purchase-
money of our religious light and freedom. They would never have
been found in the sphere of danger but for the name of Jesus Christ:
they would have discovered creditable opportunity to slink away, if
they had not loved His service better than life. Do you think their
quietly-heroic example nothing to this age? . . . How shall we measure
the influence of life laid down for Jesus Christ? Thanks be to God for
the martyrs! . . .

In one closing word, I remind you of Christ's appeal to His people
through the missionary enterprise—the appeal that comes most directly
and powerfully home to the Christian heart. He understood us best. He
does not allure us with the promise of a terrestrial paradise, or this

world's renown. He looks forth into our midst—looks into this gathering today—looks into our eyes with those eyes that closed in death to save us, and asks: *Who among you will die for Me?*

> James Culross, M.A., D.D., 'To What Purpose Is This Waste?', Mount Pleasant Chapel, Swansea, October 1885, in *Missionary Sermons* (1924), 135-45

G Missionary testimonies

I thank God most sincerely and devoutly that I am a missionary. I never regretted the step I took many years ago; and if there is a sincere desire burning within my breast, it is that I may live and die in labouring and suffering for Christ among the heathen. Oh, it is a glorious work! I know no work like it—so real, so unselfish, so apostolic, so Christ-like. I know no work that brings Christ so near to the soul, that throws a man back so completely on God, and that makes the grand old Gospel appear so real, so precious, so divine. And, then, think of the grandeur of our aim! Our cry is, 'China for Christ! India for Christ! the world for Christ!' Think of China and her hundreds of millions becoming our Lord's and His Christ's! Is there nothing grand in that idea? Is there nothing soul-stirring in the prospect? Is that not an achievement worthy of the best efforts of the Church, and of the noblest powers of the most richly endowed among you? And then think of the unspeakable privilege and honour of having a share in a work destined to such glorious issues. Oh, young men, think of it, dwell upon it; and if you hear the voice of God calling you, manfully take up your cross and go, and you will never cease to thank Jesus Christ our Lord for counting you worthy to be missionaries. . . .

Take your Bible, and carefully count, not the chapters or verses, but the *letters* from the beginning of Genesis to the 'Amen' of the Revelation; and when you have accomplished the task, go over it again and again and again—ten times, twenty times, forty times, nay, you must read the very letters of your Bible *eighty* times over before you have reached the requisite sum. It would take something like the letters of eighty Bibles to represent the men, women and children of that old and wondrous Empire of China. Fourteen hundred of them have sunk into Christless graves during the last hour; thirty-three thousand will pass today forever beyond your reach. Despatch your missionary tomorrow, and one million and a quarter of immortal souls, for whom Christ died, will have passed to their final account before he can reach their shores. Whether such facts touch us or not, I think they ought to move our hearts. It is enough to make an angel weep.

> Missionary testimonies of the Reverend Griffith John and the Reverend Silvester Whitehead, cited in M. G. Guinness, *The Story of the China Inland Mission* (1900), Volume I, 46; Volume II, 2

H The social implications of Christian missions

When the gospel changed their hearts, it softened their manners, and enlightened their understandings. Finding their religion to be false, they suspected that everything else by which they had been ruled must be wrong—their customs, their manners, their legislation. Hence, at their *paraprouras*, or conversations for improvement, instituted by the missionaries, they would freuqently solicit information, not on moral and religious subjects only, but also on government and juris-prudence. The missionaries, however, always referred them to the kings and the chiefs, when questions of policy were put to them, saying that they came not thither to meddle with the laws and civil institutions, but to teach them the true religion, which would itself prepare them to receive and practise what was true, and right and good in every other respect. At length the king himself requested their assistance in forming a new code of laws, founded on scriptural authority and principles. Even this they declined as long as they could with propriety, but being often importuned, they consented to prepare a code of legislation, suited to the changed circumstances of the people. . . .

Since the new settlement has begun, the character and manners of the people have been rapidly and happily changed; they are becoming more and more industrious, orderly and clean, as well as more intelligent and willing to be instructed in the things that pertain to godliness, finding it profitable to this life, in addition to the promise of the life to come. Many well-framed and plaistered houses have been built, and domestic accommodations unknown to their ancestors are found under every roof. . . .

While these village-erections are thus going forward, a new form of society is growing up with them. The advantages of neighbourly intercourse and religious instruction, tend to localize the settlers, and to wean them from their vagrant habits of strolling from place to place, and eating idle bread wherever they could get it. The gospel may be said to have first taught them the calm, enduring and endearing

sweets of home, which their vagabond forefathers, and many of themselves, hardly knew to exist, till the religion of Him who had not where
to lay his head, taught them how good and pleasant a thing it is for
brethren to dwell together in unity, instead of roving like fishes or
littering like swine.

We also observe, with great satisfaction, that Christianity, so far
from destroying those distinctions in social life, which a wise Providence
has made so necessary to human happiness, that no barbarians are
entirely without them, has both sanctioned and sanctified them here.
The kings and chiefs were never held in higher esteem by their subjects
and dependants then they are now; nor are the gradations of rank in
any part of Europe more easily recognized in these uttermost parts of
the sea. . . .

When deacons were to be appointed, though Mahine, Hautia and
other principal persons were really the best qualified for the responsible
trust, both by their talents and devotedness to the service of God, yet
—from an apprehension that it might form a dangerous precedent, and
be pleaded thereafter as authority why their successors in the kingly
dignity should also be chosen to this office in the church; and, likewise,
lest temporal chiefs should imagine that their rank gave them right to
lord it over God's heritage—the Missionaries conscientiously opposed
the election of deacons from that class. To the honour of those who
were thus passed by, they all had the good sense to acknowledge the
validity of such an objection, and the good feeling not to be offended,
but meekly to submit to the decision of those in whom they confided,
not only as their spiritual fathers, but as their best counsellors in matters
concerning which they deemed it right to interpose with their advice;
and the interference of the Missionaries in peculiar cases, like the present,
being never either officious or impertinent, has always carried weight
and influence in proportion. Under the idolatrous system, the kings had
uniformly been chief-priests; and it required no little firmness to prevent a similar association of secular and ecclesiastical preeminence
being introduced into Christian institutions. In the places of common
worship, therefore, kings, chiefs, raatiras and people, meet as equals;
but elsewhere, we may affirm from what we have seen, in no country is
greater respect and obedience paid to civil authorities.

James Montgomery (ed.), *Journal of the
Voyages and Travels of Daniel Tyerman and
George Bennet deputed from the London Mis-
sionary Society in the South Sea Islands etc.*,
Volume I (1831), 92–3, 202–4, 292–3

I   The political implications of Christian missions

(i)   Knibb's instructions

'You are quite aware', says Mr Dyer, 'that the state of society in Jamaica is very different from that under which it is our privilege to live in this country, and that the great majority of its inhabitants are dependent upon their superiors in a degree altogether unknown here. The evidence of the fact will probably, especially at first, be painful and trying to your feelings; but you must ever bear in mind that, as a resident in Jamaica, you have nothing whatever to do with its civil or political affairs, and with these you must never interfere. Your simple object is, first, to attend to the instruction of the children placed under your care, and then to render such assistance to Mr Coultart in his ministerial duties as appear desirable, and as may be permitted by the local authorities. These engagements, we conceive, will fully occupy your time and strength, and, in confining yourself to them, as we charge you always to do, you cannot justly incur the displeasure of those among whom you may be placed. The Gospel of Christ, you well know, so far from producing or countenancing a spirit of rebellion or insubordination, has a directly opposite tendency. Most of the servants addressed by the apostle Paul in his epistles were slaves, and he exhorts them to be obedient to their masters, in singleness of heart, fearing God; and this not only to the good and gentle, but also to the forward. Let your instructions, both to young and old, be conceived in the spirit, and correspond with the directions and example, of our Divine Teacher, as laid down in the New Testament at large; and then, whatever disposition may be felt to obstruct or misrepresent you, none will justly be able to lay anything to your charge.' . . .

(ii)   Knibb's own confession

'For my own part, I shall not shrink from those duties which I owe to my people. As soon as it became known that the apprenticeship was to cease, I used every means in my power, in connection with my friends of other denominations to bring about a proper feeling between employers and labourers. . . .

It has been said that I am the friend of the black man only. I deny it; but I deny also the right of having our sympathies called forth for the white man at the expense of the negro. I sympathize with the oppressed, whether he be black or white. This is no political meeting. In fact I do not exactly know what is called a political meeting in this country. Politics, to me, are altogether inexplicable; they are like a round ball, you can never find the end. I have called this meeting for the purpose of telling my people what I consider is calculated to prevent imposition, and I should be unworthy of the trust reposed in me by them, if I did not interfere. I pledge myself, by all that is solemn and sacred, never to rest satisfied, until I see my black brethren in the enjoyment of the same civil and religious liberties which I myself enjoy, and see them take a proper stand in society as men.... Let the enemies of liberty secretly combine as they please; let them endeavour to oppress the peasant as they formerly trampled on the slave; we tell them they shall not succeed. With the omnipotence of a British parliament, with the voice of a free nation, with a governor who feels the worth of the people he governs, with a noble band of patriots engaged on our side, and, with the blessing of heaven, we must prevail. Maintain the character, my Christian friends, that you have hitherto maintained. Be honest, be industrious, and your example shall speed the sacred cause of freedom. Be assured that in your ministers you will still find friends, who, while they point you to the Lamb of God as the only atonement for sin, will at the same time protect you from every wrong, so far as they are able. The advocates of oppression cannot stop the march of liberty. Onward, onward, is the watchword. The whole earth has caught the delightful sound, and the time is not far distant when the sun will not shine on a tyrant, or on a slave.'

J. H. Hinton, Memoir of William Knibb (1847),
149–50, 286–91

J Missionaries and the Empire

Behind every new missionary effort there is somewhere a new Pentecost—a grand reception hour when Heaven opens to send down a fuller measure of grace, and the heart of the Church is wonderfully enlarged to take it in. Behind Carey there are Wesleys and Whitefields and the Evangelical revival. Behind the Moravian missions there was that wonderful opening of the heart to the Holy Ghost known as German pietism. Behind even the Jesuit missions there was a strange new revelation given to a few men like Xavier and Loyola of the entrancing beauty of Jesus. Behind every forward movement there is an inrush of Cross power and of the Holy Ghost; immense gladness, a

Church thrilling, throbbing, excited, and burning with the consciousness of its privileges and the sweets of Jesus' love. . . .

Our receipts make our debt. The Lord tells us here, and His words
are echoed in all the confessions of His disciples, that we have received
for the very purpose of giving. The Gospel has been committed to us in
trust. We are not absolute owners, we are responsible trustees. . . .

If it has not yet penetrated and suffused the hearts of all Christians,
it is because the selfish human elements have counteracted the workings
of the Divine, and because man's littleness has brought God's great
thought down to the measure of the market and the shop. It must be
felt by those whom Christ has lifted above the commercial atmosphere. . . .

Pardon me, if for a moment I extend this thought of obligation to a
wider field. It touches the nation. Nay, it should press upon the nation.
The very reason that makes us thankful and proud to bear the British
name should beget in us a deep, solemn, prayerful sense of responsibility and debt towards the less privileged races of the world. Freely
have ye received, indeed! There is nothing more wonderful in the story
of empires and nations, and nothing more unaccountable by ordinary
causes, than the growth in power, wealth, and influence of our own
people and of the people who share our language and religion. What
vanity would have dared to project the dream which our eyes see
realized. Who would have believed it possible that the kingdom of
Elizabeth would expand into the empire of Victoria; that the dear,
dear land whose praises Shakespeare sang would strengthen its stakes
and enlarge the places of its tent until its sons ruled over one-third of
the human race?

Imagine some prophet writing in those days when this little island
was overshadowed by France, dreading conquest by Spain, soon to be
outstripped in commercial power by Holland. Imagine him borrowing
the words of Scripture and saying: 'Thou shalt break forth on the right
hand and on the left, and thy seed shall inherit the Gentiles, and make
the desolate places to be inhabited. The abundance of the sea shall be
converted unto thee, the forces of the Gentiles shall come unto thee,
and the sons of strangers shall build up thy walls, and kings shall
minister unto thee.' What laughter would have attended his foolish
arrogance and insolent misappropriation of Divine words. Who would
have believed that in this short time the words would come true—that
the feeble, sea-girt people would become the mother of empires,
would carry their flag to all parts of the habitable globe, would give
their speech to some two hundred millions of lips, and bring far more

than that number of people under their authority? Think of our enormous wealth, the bankers and capitalists of the world, lending to all and borrowing from none, with an annual income at least a thousand times as much as our whole expenditure on foreign missions; think how the purity of Evangelic truth has been preserved through all manner of revolution and upheavals; how the Bible, which in other even nominally Christian lands is a closed or neglected book, is among us the book loved best, the well-nigh universal household treasure; and think how, while in nearly all Protestant lands save where our language is spoken religion is feeble or apathetic, and in Catholic lands given up by nearly all the men of culture and leading [sic], it is here full of life, power and earnestness. Think of it all. It is the one great modern miracle.

And what is the meaning of it? Do we interpret it with the boastful Jingoism of the music-hall, or with the humbler patriotism of the sanctuary? Have we got all this glory by our own might and power, or is it because He has 'beset us behind and before, and laid His hand upon us'? Can you suppose that all this wealth and influence and privilege have been conferred upon the nation for its own immediate and exclusive enjoyment, and for no wider and higher purpose? . . . Surely we have not been endowed by God in this way that we might grow fat and luxurious, or use our power over millions of subject children for our own aggrandizement, and to puff ourselves out with pride. Was it not especially with this intent—that we should be more than all others God's messengers of light and truth to the nations that sit in darkness? In all this God's voice has been calling us. . . .

We are elect by all signs and proofs to be the great missionary nation. And, alas! if we deny this high duty, or neglect it for meaner, baser, or more selfish aims; if we worship not God, but gold; if we think only of empires and ambition, and not at all of this sacred trust and obligation, our privileges will be taken from us in spite of all our ships and money and men; our wealth will decay when it has done its work of morally corrupting us; our very religion will perish, for Christ will remove the light from the candlestick which had burned only for itself. . . .

It is possible, indeed, that in the counsels of God, yes, I say it, though it may be ridiculed in some quarters, every new missionary we send out is doing more than every new ironclad we build to maintain and perpetuate the greatness of the empire. For the ultimate arbiter in these things is not battalions and ships, but He who uses nations as His instruments and rejects them when they have ceased to do His work.

You cannot, you dare not, say: 'We will have no part in this mission work; it is no interest of ours.' You dare not say it as Englishmen, still less can you say it as Christians. For not to give forth what God has given you is to annul the condition on which He gives everything.

> J. G. Greenhough, M.A., 'The Missionary Obligation', Bloomsbury Chapel, London, April 1896 in *Missionary Sermons* (1924), 255–66

K Missionary motivation: a *fin-de-siècle* view

Within the last two years the influence of the native Church, and of the ideas which are propagated by the Christian mission, has been making itself felt in the most far-reaching and conspicuous way. You have heard much of the 'Reform party' in China, of its struggles and its martyrs, and of the bitter hatred which it has drawn upon itself from all the forces of reaction. Its ideas have laid hold of the highest circles of influence, and of some of the ablest men of official rank. . . . While these movements bear on the face of them more of a political than a religious aspect, they are undoubtedly the outcome of the Christian leaven which has been working for so many years almost unseen and frequently denied by shallow observers, but whose working has nevertheless been the strongest of all the influences that are combining to shape the future destinies of China. . . . We long earnestly to see tokens that the great mass of heathen society is being reached and influenced by our teaching, and by the character of those who have already accepted it; but, while we do so, we ought never to shut our eyes to the tremendous seriousness of the work on which we are engaged. It is no doubt in our immediate intention the work of saving individual souls, of leading them to a purer life here and a happy life hereafter, but it is a work also which tells with enormous power and with consequences which we are wholly unable to calculate, upon national life and destiny. The question must sometimes press itself upon thoughtful minds in view of the great issues of such work as this, 'Have we any right to disturb the life of nations by the introduction among them of such enormous forces, and, in view of the dangers involved, is it worthwhile?' The question is well answered in words once used by Principal Rainy in a public address: 'It is worth while, *if we mean it*: it is worthwhile, if for ourselves Christ is the one necessity of our hearts.' Those who undertake to carry on mission work amongst great peoples, undertake great responsibilities. We have no right to penetrate these nations with a revolutionary Gospel of enormous power unless we are prepared also to make every sacrifice and every effort for the proper care, and the wise training of the Christian community itself, which, while, it must become increasingly a source of revolutionary thought and movement, is also the one body that can by the help and grace of God give these far-reaching movements a healthy direction, and lead them to safe and happy issues. . . .

I have tried to give you some idea of the moral and spiritual condition of these great multitudes of people, and in this connection I must refer shortly to one question of profound difficulty. You have often seen appeals on behalf of missions based on the plea that all the innumerable multitudes of heathens who die without hearing the Gospel must perish everlastingly. Is this a principal motive? I wish, gentlemen, that I could honestly pass by this profoundly difficult question. . . . It is a question which must lie heavily on the spirit of every missionary, and cannot be long absent from his mind. It is one thing to reason in the abstract about multitudes and millions far away; it is quite another when one is thinking of the laughing boys and girls, the hearty, kindly young men, the weary old men and burdened women, among whom one is living, and from whom one has times without number received the little kindnesses and courtesies which even in a heathen country are so often shown to the passing stranger.

I feel bound to say to you that whatever conclusion one might be driven to by irresistible convinction, I at least could never speak of the belief that all heathen men and women and children who do not hear the Gospel are inevitably doomed to eternal death, as a motive to the work of missions. On the contrary—'that way, madness lies'—this doctrine, if it forced itself without any conceivable alleviation on my mind, would utterly paralyse me. It would weigh with crushing force, and could never be to me a spring or motive for action.

J. Campbell Gibson, *Mission Problems and
Mission Methods In South China* (1901), 164–6,
229–30, 275–7, 322–3

L Joint enterprise

. . . We cordially rejoice in the prosperity of all missions set on foot by real believers in Christ Jesus. And our brethren in India have uniformly discovered a spirit of kindness towards their fellow-labourers sent out by other societies. Nor is there anything for which I more sincerely

and earnestly pray than that both they and we may ever be kept from
all party-spirit, from all self-seeking, and from all self-confidence and
vain boasting.

Never, indeed, may we listen to that spurious moderation, which
requires a dereliction of principle, or a disregard to what we believe to
be most agreeable to the word of God: but never may we lay an undue
stress on those things wherein they may differ who worship God in
the spirit, rejoice in Christ Jesus, and have no confidence in the flesh.
All who love our Lord Jesus Christ in sincerity shall share in our love;
all who appear to be led by the Spirit of God shall be acknowledged as
the children of God, and as our dear brethren; yet we will follow none
of them farther than we see them following the footsteps of Christ.
But nothing in which bad men can possibly unite shall unite us so
closely as those things in which good men cannot disagree.

> John Ryland, D.D., 'The Zeal of the Lord of
> Hosts', Dutch Church, London, June 1812, in
> *Missionary Sermons* (1924), 26

M The Evangelical Alliance

(i) *A mid-century union*

The Rev. Dr Wardlaw: In connection with the great movement for
Christian Union, there are two very pleasing facts, of which they had
visible assurance by looking round upon that Meeting—the fact of
Variety, and the fact of Unity. The fact of Variety existed in two forms
—variety of sentiment and variety of locality. They were of different
Christian denominations—would to God the term had never been
originated! He presumed that there were then present the representa-
tives of not less, perhaps more, than twenty different Evangelical
Christian denominations. He might also say, that since denominational
Christianity began, there had never been such a manifestation at once
of its Variety and Unity, as they saw before them at that moment.
Their variety of sentiment was a great fact . . . and yet the fact of their
unity was equally evident. They felt that they were one . . .

The Rev. Dr W. Symington: This forgetting or banishing or merging
or getting rid of our differences is not a theory. If I may refer to my own
experience, as a respected Brother did this morning, I would say I
realized this at the bi-centenary Commemoration of the Westminster
Assembly three years ago. We met there under peculiar circumstances:
it was immediately after the heat of the Voluntary controversy, in

which we had been pitted together for years. We read the Scriptures of truth, we sang the praises of God, we joined in prayer, we read essays in one another's hearing. And the result was, although I had taken part in the controversy, and though I did not feel that I had compromised my principles, that I could not for my life have said a bitter thing of any one Member with whom I had been associated there . . .

Proposition: 'That in subserviency to the grand object already intimated, the expectation is cherished, that the Alliance will exert a beneficial influence on the advancement of Christianity in various important respects: such as counter-acting the efforts of Popery, and other forms of superstition and infidelity, and promoting their common Protestant Faith in this and other countries; and that, with this view, it is deemed necessary to obtain correct information, on such subjects as the following, namely—

1. The facts bearing on the growth of Popery.
2. The state of Infidelity, and the form which it assumes at the present day.
3. The facts relating to the Public Observance of the Lord's Day.
4. The amount of the existing means of Christian education.

It being understood that, in the following up of the enquiries to be thus made, and in promoting these and similar objects, the Alliance contemplates chiefly the stimulating of Christians to such efforts as the exigencies of the case may demand, by giving forth its views in regard to them . . .

The Rev. Thomas Binney: There are several additional subjects of great importance which I should like to see brought out. There is the question of Public Morals. There are many facts, I think, in connection with Public Morals, a great Evangelical and Christian Society like ours might touch upon with delicacy and power . . . books, spread out for sale, many of them obviously and manifestly translations from the French, of a very infamous description. . . . Then there is the 'observance of the Lord's Day'. . . . Then there is 'Temperance'. . . . There are many things in which I should desire to see more of union and communion . . .

The Rev. Arthur Tidman: I am quite sure, with regard to the general principle to which I am now speaking, that any thing in this Alliance which should bear any resemblance to Anti-Popish aggression would greatly wound us, and would prevent the co-operation of multitudes, whom it is desirous to conciliate and bring into this bond of brotherly affection. I see some gentlemen shaking their heads, and I have no

right to call upon them to believe what I affirm; but I have some
knowledge of many who have hitherto held back from this Association, and I know, that were there the slightest approach to such a
character as the proceedings of yesterday threatened, it would go very
far to deprive us of their future assistance. . .

   The Rev. J. H. Hinton: Since, as in any part of the world, an adhesion
to the general principles and objects of the Alliance qualifies for Member-
ship, it admits of no doubt that some members in the United States
Branch will be slave-holders. I am entitled, I suppose, to affirm this . . .
by the fact that some of the American brethren here are pastors of
Slave-holding Churches—that is, of Churches admitting Slaveholders.
So that it is not a thing to be doubted, that, according to this General
Organization, there will be slave-holders, members of the Alliance.
Now, sir, the degree of association and connection into which all
members of the Alliance will soon be brought, is such that for my
part (and many others agree with me)—as I cannot assent to the recognition of the Christian character and standing of Slaveholders—so I
cannot, in my conscience give to them the privilege of membership.

*Evangelical Alliance: Report of the Proceedings of
the Conference Held at London,* August–
September 1846 (1847), 44, 197–8, 240, 262–3,
291

(ii) *A Dissentient view*

We look with considerable apprehension to the 'objects' which the
Alliance may be disposed to take up. Such an organization must be too
vast, and must be constituted of elements much too diverse, to be
competent to much practical action. There will be sharp war during the
present century, between Romanism and Protestantism; and a still
hotter conflict so far as regards the educated classes, between Revealed
Religion and the Literary Pantheism which is now everywhere taking
hold on the literature of Europe. But the Evangelical Alliance will not
be the power to grapple with these evils. Churchmen and Dissenters are
not agreed as to the true grounds of controversy with the Church
of Rome. In both connections also, the difference between the educated
and uneducated is such as must prevent their seeing alike as to what
should be conceded, and what should be denied, in respect to the infidel,
or semi-infidel theories of the age. Such labours may be better left to
smaller and less responsible organizations, and best of all to that spirit
of private enterprise which on questions of this nature, rarely fails of

being equal to the demand. On such subjects as we have mentioned, even the speech-making of the Alliance would be likely we fear to do more harm than good; and to its publications in relation to such topics we should look with a most painful distrust.

British Quarterly Review, Volume 3 (1846), 533-4

N Free Church unity

(i) *A confident rationale*

The astonishing unanimity and ease with which one of the most novel and far-reaching movements of our time has assumed national proportions are due to two causes.

First of all the entire disappearance of our own internal differences. In the early days of the Reformation there was not much love lost between the Presbyterians, the Congregationalists and the Society of Friends. When those ancient Dissenters settled down into friendly relations with one another, the advent of Methodism produced a fresh controversy. . . . Now like Wesley and Whitefield we all 'agree to differ' on points of interpretation while we realize our fundamental agreement on the essential facts of the Christian religion. This astonishing theological calm is something so totally new in our ecclesiastical history and has been brought about so gradually and unintentionally that not only do we deserve no credit for it, but it has scarcely yet received even from ourselves the consideration it deserves. . . .

The second cause of the Movement we represent is a very different and a very sad one. It is the portentous revival in our midst of extreme medieval clericalism which our fathers believed had disappeared for ever from England. Some of the most conspicuous, influential and energetic of the Anglican clergy now advocate clerical dogmas and practise clerical arts which would have shocked even Archbishop Laud himself. . . . We are quite sure Mr Benjamin Kidd expressed the historic truth when in his remarkable 'Social Evolution' he declared that God gave the civilized nations of Europe their great opportunity in the sixteenth century; that those of them which then turned their back upon the higher ethical standard of the Reformation have been sinking lower and lower ever since; and that those of them on the other hand which then responded to the great call of God have from that epoch-making age until now been rising higher and higher in the scale of empire, civilization, freedom and progress. The disappearance of our own internal differences is the negative cause of our acting together; but the positive cause is our unanimous determination that, God helping us, England, the land of civil and religious freedom, the land of Gospel light, shall never sink to the degraded level of Spain.

All that I have just said tends to define the nature of the Movement today. In the first place and emphatically, it is not a 'political' movement in the sense in which that greatly abused word is usually employed. . . . The Church of Rome and the Church of England have been almost wrecked again and again by the folly of their ecclesiastical rulers in identifying them with the interests of a particular political party. God forbid that we should ever imitate their suicidal example. . . . Each issue must be considered on its merits. So long as any public question fiercely divides us and is calculated to destroy our internal unity, it would be suicidal for us to touch it. But there are great causes, such as the Temperance Movement, the Purity Movement, the Anti-gambling Movement and the Peace Movement which, although they have their political sides are essentially moral and Christian, and which, without fear of internal discard, we must promote with all our might.

In the next place this Movement is not merely a civic or philanthropic movement, or we should heartily welcome the co-operation of all good citizens on the broad basis of our common humanity. It is distinctly a Christian and ecclsiastical movement. That is its characteristic note. It is not like the Church Congress, a fortuitous concourse of atoms, representing simply personal opinion, and attaching importance to numbers. . . . Further we are not like the Evangelical Alliance, a mere gathering of individual Christians expressing occasional sympathy with one another, but a federation of organized churches as such. . . .

I come now to consider the specific objects of this organized ecclesia-stical Movement. The Constitution which the last Congress ordered the Committee to prepare, and to the preparation of which the Committee has devoted many hours . . . emphasizes in brief but pregnant terms the objects of the movement. The first is 'to facilitate and promote fraternal intercourse among the Evangelical Free Churches'. One of the most mischievous, although best recognized, evils of our unhappy divisions is the fragmentary narrowness of thought and sympathy they inevitably cause. . . . I believe that our future and the future of the British Empire and therefore to a great extent the future of the human race depends under God on the extent to which the Churches we represent are able to distinguish between denominational loyalty and bigotry, between denominational independence and sectarianism, between denominational activity and schism. Can we rise above small ideals and narrow ambitions?

And so I pass naturally to the second great object that we set before ourselves—the deepening of our own spiritual life. . . . We are confronted in every part of this country by a vast Unreached Majority of the people. In every city, town and village, the great majority are outside all Churches. . . . During the last year at Birmingham and elsewhere, some of our local Councils have shown us a splendid example of the way in which the Free Evangelical Churches can unite in aggressive evangelistic work on a massive scale. . . . A great deal of excellent evangelistic work has been undertaken in our time by what I must call scratch committees of well-meaning Christians united casually and exclusively for that purpose. When such a mission is over, the committee disappears, and a great deal of the result disappears with it. Jesus Christ came into this world not merely to save individuals but also to organize a Christian Church that should care for 'babes in Christ', which babes need every kind of protection and nurture. . . . No aggressive attempt to bring men to Christian decision has in it a rational or scriptural guarantee of permanence unless it is based upon the organized fellowship of the Christian Church. . . .

I now come to the most novel, the most characteristic and the most necessary part of our appointed work. The Constitution, which you will consider tomorrow, suggests that one essential object of this Movement should be 'to advocate the New Testament doctrine of the Church'.

It is high time we made a more positive statement of our Faith. What are we? We are Free Evangelical Churchmen. Above all, we are Churchmen. We are in truth, High Churchmen, and the highest of all Churchmen, so high that we could not think for a moment of allowing any politician to appoint our ministers or any parliament to manipulate our creed. . . . We are not one in the Pope. We are not one in the Crown. But we are one in Christ. The Roman Catholic stands for the supremacy of the Pope, the Anglican Catholic for the supremacy of the Crown, and the Scriptural Catholic for the supremacy of Christ. That is our point of union, and we realize it more and more. The late Dr Dale delivered an invaluable lecture on 'Protestantism, its Ultimate Principle' . . . Dr Dale proves that the ultimate principle of Protestantism is neither the right of private judgment nor the authority of Holy Scripture, nor Justification by faith, but the unique and supreme authority of Jesus Christ. . . . The fact is that a really enlightened Protestant puts neither the Church nor the Bible between himself and Christ. His supreme faith is neither in an infallible Church nor an infallible Bible, but an infallible Christ. . . .

Finally we may sum up our deepest convictions in the memorable words, which were the personal confession of our own great Nonconformist poet, Robert Browning—

I say, the acknowledgement of God in Christ
Accepted by thy reason, solves for thee
All questions in the earth or out of it.

That expresses our creed and our programme. Our vocation, in real and happy association with one another, is to 'seek first the kingdom of God and his righteousness'—the reconstruction both of human society and of personal life on a Christian basis. . . .

Our divisions and our disunions have concealed our real strength from ourselves and others. If we look abroad our resources become yet more encouraging. Representing a majority of the Christian people at home, we represent an immense majority in the British Empire, and an overwhelming majority in the English-speaking world. If the failures and humiliations of the past, as well as the bright hopes of the present have at last taught us their Divinely-appointed lessons, the future of British Christianity and of the British Empire is in our hands. In the most important and influential quarters of the globe, we can under God build up a Holy, Catholic and Apostolic Church, we can decisively influence the course of human events, we can greatly hasten the advent of the blissful day.

> *Proceedings of the First National Council of the Evangelical Free Churches* (1896). Presidential Address by Hugh Price Hughes, 24–38

(ii) *A painful analysis*

. . . it is easy to point to a number of respectable persons who have recently left the 'chapel' and gone to the 'church'. Who can question that a large proportion of the Dissenters who attain wealth and social position become Churchmen, or at any rate, attendants at Church? And if they do not take the decisive step themselves, their sons and daughters take it, not without their encouragement, so that they enjoy the double benefit of clinging to their own convictions and basking in social sunshine because their children have been fortunate enough to lose theirs.

I fall back therefore on the assertions of able and religious editors and on the reports of triumphant correspondents, and accept the position that Dissent is about to disappear, and that, what Laud failed to do by his Court of High Commission, the Church is on the point of accomplishing by its 'sweetness and light', its 'unity', its disinterestedness, its devotion and the happy command of the social rewards which the English desire. Admitting however that the new 'short way with Dissenters' will soon be crowned with success, it occurs to me, and to some others, to ask what may be the effect upon our national life and well-being? . . . Can we imagine the country without them? Are we sure that their disappearance will be a national gain? . . . [There follows a review of the contribution of Dissenters to the commerce, literature and life of the nation, and of ex-Dissenters to the Established Church.] I venture to make a challenge. Examine in any parish throughout the country the clergy, the teachers, the visitors, the workers who are doing anything for the real progress of religion, and if your experiences are like mine, you will find that about half of them are Dissenters by origin. In the free and strenuous life of the non-episcopal churches they have acquired the grit and developed the powers which they now devote to the service of the Established Church. . . .

Reunion may come in a moment, and in the most unexpected way, as soon as the Church of England sees, with Canon Henson, that Nonconformists also are Christians, enjoying the favour of Christ and the grace of the Holy Spirit; and with Bishop Gott, that 'the societies of Nonconformity' have taken their due part in the shaping and Christianization of England. . . .

In Hampstead I never heard any sighing for the social advantages of the Establishment, or any complaint of the ostracism involved in Dissent. The population is so largely outside all the Churches that the Churches are virtually lost in the mass which, though they do not leaven it, forms a kind of embedding material separating them one from another.

Not only would the aggressive work within the district (with reunion) become practicable, but forces would be liberated which might cope with the social evils of London, and with the vast problem of missions to the heathen. . . .

Let it be granted that the Free Churches would benefit by closer intercourse with the Established Church, and would learn the decorum and refinement in worship, and the sober moderation of the Spirit which have been the boast of Anglicanism from the beginning; still, the Anglican Church might gain something from a closer knowledge of the Free Churches—their greater flexibility of organization and teaching, their firmer insistence on preaching and teaching as an essential in worship and their wider view of the Church. . . .

Neither the numberless defections of Dissenters with social ambitions and lukewarm faith, nor the extremes of enthusiasts and fanatics, can materially affect that vast body of Nonconformists which rests upon the truth of the New Testament, and is sustained not only by the discoveries of scholarship but also by the powerful testimony of the Spirit of God. This genuine Nonconformity is, I have contended, a priceless national possession. A wise country will not wish to be quit it of. A wise Church will desire not to crush it out, but to win it, by expanding her own conceptions of truth, and widening her borders in response to the larger vision.

R. F. Horton: *The Dissolution of Dissent* (1902),
10–11, 37, 105, 111, 142–3, 145

BOOKS FOR FURTHER READING

In the history of Victorian Nonconformity older books are not to be despised: in order to fill in the detail of the relevant chapters of E. A. Payne, *The Free Church Tradition in the Life of England* (revised edn. 1965), a student is well advised to consult one of the older histories such as H. W. Clark's *History of English Nonconformity* (2 vols. 1911–13). C. Driver, in *A Future for the Free Churches* (1962), relates the history of the immediate past to present prospects.

General works which have much to say about nineteenth-century Dissent are Horton Davies' *Worship and Theology in England* (vols. III and IV 1961–2); Kathleen Heaseman's enthusiastic *Evangelicals in Action* (1962); K. S. Inglis, *Churches and the Working Classes in Victorian England* (1963); S. Mayor, *The Churches and the Labour Movement* (1967) and J. D. Gay, *The Geography of Religion in England* (1971).

Particular topics are dealt with by B. L. Manning, *The Protestant Dissenting Deputies* (1952); W. B. Glover, *Evangelical Nonconformity and Higher Criticism in the Nineteenth Century* (1954); H. F. Lovell Cocks, *The Nonconformist Conscience* (1943); J. E. Orr, *The Second Evangelical Awakening in Britain* (1949). J. W. Grant in *Free Churchmanship in England, 1870–1900* (n.d., c. 1950), gives an account of developments in ecclesiastical theology with special attention to Congregationalists.

O. Beckerlegge, *The United Methodist Free Churches* (1951), and T. Shaw, *The Bible Christians*, (1965), give recent accounts of these parts of the Methodist tradition, but for Primitive Methodism one is still dependent upon H. B. Kendall, *History of the Primitive Methodist Church* (revised edn. 1919). Similarly, until the second volume of R. Davies and E. G. Rupp, *A History of the Methodist Church in Great Britain* (1966), appears, one is still dependent for the nineteenth century upon W. S. Townsend, H. B. Workman and G. Eayrs, *A New History of Methodism* (2 vols. 1909). R. F. Wearmouth tells an important story, perhaps a little unguardedly, in *Methodism and the Working-class movements of England, 1800–1850* (1937) and *Methodism and the Struggle of the Working classes 1850–1909* (1955). Recent studies of Methodism include John Kent's *The Age of Disunity* (1966) and R. Currie, *Methodism Divided* (1965).

The Congregational story has been retold by R. T. Jones in *Congregationalism in England 1662–1962* (1962), but E. A. Payne, *The Baptist Union, a short history* (1959), confines itself to looking out from the denominational headquarters: for the larger story resort still needs to be made to A. C. Underwood, *A History of English Baptists* (1947).

Quakers have been well served by Mrs E. Isichei in *Victorian Quakers* (1970), but the Unitarian symposium C. G. Bolam et al., *The English Presbyterians* (1968), is less satisfactory, and needs to be supplemented by R. V. Holt, *The Unitarian Contribution to Social Progress in England* (2nd. edn. 1952).

Much of the detailed history is to be found in the periodicals of the various Free Church Historical Societies and files of the following should be consulted: *Baptist Quarterly*, *Transactions of the Congregational Historical Society*, *Friends Historical Society Journal*, *The Journal of the Presbyterian Historical Society of England*, *Transactions of the Unitarian Historial Society* and *Proceedings of the Wesley Historical Society*.

Perhaps the best way to take the subject further is, however, through biography, especially those great red-bound biographies of so many of the principal Victorian Nonconformists that Hodder and Stoughton produced in the early years of this century: here is a rich mine, readily accessible, which will repay careful study.

Finally, the editors of the present volume have to note that two volumes on similar themes appeared after the present text had been completed: E. Royle, *Radical Politics, 1790–1900, Religion and Unbelief* and D. Thompson, *Nonconformity in the nineteenth century*. The same is also true of Professor W. R. Ward's provocative study; *Religion and Society in England, 1790–1850*.

BIOGRAPHICAL NOTE

HENRY ALLON (1818–92): Minister of Union Chapel, Islington from 1844 to 1892. Twice Chairman of the Congregational Union (in 1864 and 1881) he was particularly concerned to encourage scholarship and high musical and liturgical standards amongst Congregationalists. In 1866 he succeeded Robert Vaughan as a joint editor of the *British Quarterly Review* and from 1874 to its demise twelve years later was its sole editor. The correspondence he received in this office has been edited by Albert Peel (*Letters to a Victorian Editor*, 1929) affording the scholar valuable evidence as to the interaction between Nonconformity and the late Victorian generation.

JOSEPH ANGUS (1816–1902): A distinguished academic career at Edistburgh, a London pastorate, and the Secretaryship of the Baptin Missionary Society (1840–49) preceded his appointment as President of Stepney, subsequently Regent's Park, College (1849–93). In 1870 he was appointed to both the New Testament Panel for the revision of the authorized version of the Bible and to the first London School Board.

R. A. ARMSTRONG (1843–1906): Unitarian divine with notable pastorates in Nottingham (1869–83) and Liverpool (1883–1905) where he preached a Wordsworthian form of 'cosmic theism'. Implementing the 'social gospel' he also campaigned for 'Municipal Morality'.

EDWARD BAINES (1800–1890): Son of a popular MP for Leeds he began editing the *Leeds Mercury* at the age of 18. In the 1840s he articulated the Voluntaryist view of education which dominated Congregationalist thinking for many years. He himself was MP for Leeds from 1859–74. Tireless as a philanthropist, he was knighted in 1880.

CHARLES BEARD (1827–88): Studied at Manchester, London and Berlin and was successively Unitarian minister at Hyde, Cheshire and in Liverpool. A notable spokesman for Unitarianism, he was an active political journalist until the Liberal party adopted Home Rule. He became a Vice-President of University College, Liverpool.

J. BALDWIN BROWN (1820–84): One of the first graduates of London University, he exercised a remarkable pulpit ministry in South

London from 1846 in favour of what might be called 'Broad-Church Congregationalism'.

JOHN CLIFFORD (1836–1923): Baptist minister in Paddington from 1858. His advanced liberal politics (he was a member of the Fabian society) was accompanied by an advocacy of liberal evangelicalism. The leader of the 'passive resistance' movement after the 1902 Act, he was made a Companion of Honour in 1921.

THOMAS COOPER (1805–92): Midland Chartist leader, editor and writer; in his early life a Wesleyan lay-preacher he became first an apostle of free thought, and then a Baptist defender of orthodoxy.

R. W. DALE (1829–95): After taking a London M.A. with a gold medal in philosophy in 1853, he became co-pastor at Carr's Lane, Birmingham and sole pastor from 1859. He refused many invitations to other appointments giving himself instead entirely to involvement in Birmingham. Chairman of the Congregational Union in 1869 he withdrew from it in 1888 over Home Rule preferring to stand by Chamberlain and the Liberal Unionists. In 1891, however, he became first Moderator of the International Congregational Council.

P. T. FORSYTH (1848–1921): Having studied under Ritschl in Germany, was initially regarded as one of Congregationalism's most liberal young scholars. As Principal of Hackney College 1861–1921 he came more and more to articulate views which would later be called neo-orthodox.

CHARLES GARRETT (1823–1900): One of the principal founders of the Manchester and Salford Lay Mission. He, there, and in Liverpool, played a major part in leading Wesleyan Methodism into the Forward Movement of the 1880s.

ROBERT HALL (the younger) (1764–1831): A Baptist divine, who held notable pastorates in Cambridge, Leicester and Bristol.

R. F. HORTON (1855–1934): After schooling at Shrewsbury took a double first at Oxford, became President of the Union and in 1879 was elected a Fellow of New College. In the following year he began preaching in a 'tin tab' in Hampstead to which work he devoted all his time after 1883 when the Convocation of Oxford University rejected his appointment as an examiner in theology. He ministered to a large and remarkable congregation of more than a thousand at Lyndhurst Road for 50 years, and communicated with a much wider number through his writings which though sometimes controversial were always reverential.

HUGH PRICE HUGHES (1847–1902): From 1884 he became the leader of the 'Forward Movement' in Methodism, founding the *Methodist*

Times a year later. As first president of the National Free Church Council he did much to associate Wesleyan Methodists with the Free Church movement.

JOHN ANGELL JAMES (1785–1859): Minister of Carr's Lane, Birmingham (1805–59). One of the great princes of the Victorian pulpit, he wrote a widely influential tract entitled *The Anxious Enquirer* (1834). He was succeeded by R. W. Dale.

WILLIAM KNIBB (1803–45): Baptist missionary to Jamaica who became a notable advocate of the abolition of slavery.

EDWARD MIALL (1809–81) The first number of his newspaper *The Nonconformist* appeared in 1841 bearing the legend 'The Dissidence of Dissent and the Protestantism of the Protestant Religion'. Three years later he founded the British Anti-State Church Association which after 1854 became the Liberation Society. In parliament from 1852–7 and 1869–74 he led political dissent in its campaign for disestablishment.

JAMES MONTGOMERY (1771–1854): Son of a Moravian minister, he became editor of the *Sheffield Register*, (from 1794 the *Sheffield Iris*). Twice imprisoned for radical views, he retained his Moravian connections though he mainly worshipped with the Wesleyans.

DWIGHT L. MOODY (1837–99): An American Congregationalist of Unitarian stock who had close associations with the YMCA, Moody first visited England in 1867. His most famous campaign however was that of 1873–5 but was followed by further visits in 1881–4 and 1891–2. His name is indissolubly linked with that of IRA D. SANKEY (1804–1908) the hymn writer.

J. P. MURSELL (1799–1885): Baptist minister in Leicester and collaborator with Miall in the radical politics of that town and in the work of the Liberation Society.

DAVID NASMITH (1799–1839): Is notable as the originator of town and city missions starting in Glasgow, his home town, in 1826, and leading to the establishment of the London City Mission 10 years later.

JOSEPH PARKER (1830–1902): Parker moved to London in 1869 after a notable ministry in Manchester. An orthodox but dramatic preacher, the City Temple was built for him in 1874: he was twice Chairman of the Congregational Union.

HENRY RICHARD (1812–1888): Left the Congregational ministry in 1850 to work full-time for the Peace Society. In 1868–88 he was Liberal MP for the Merthyr Boroughs. A keen Liberationist he was Chairman of the Congregational Union in 1877.

J. GUINESS ROGERS (1822–1911): A graduate of Trinity College, Dublin he had outstanding pastorates in Newcastle, Ashton-under-Lyne and Clapham as well as serving as a denominational editor from 1879–1891. Along with R. W. Dale he was often consulted by Gladstone as to the 'nonconformist view'.

JOHN RYLAND (1753–1825): Baptist minister in Northampton and Bristol, he was Secretary of the Baptist Missionary Society (1793–1825).

JOHN PYE SMITH (1774–1851): Educated at Rotherham College he himself became Tutor and Principal of Homerton College. His scholarship was rewarded by the award of a D.D. from Yale, an LL.D. from Aberdeen and election as an F.R.S. A keen 'liberationist' and an ardent pacifist he became the doyen of liberal politicians amongst the ministers of his denomination.

CHARLES HADDON SPURGEON (1834–92): Came to London in 1854 and made an immediate impact as the capital's most popular preacher. The Metropolitan Tabernacle, capable of seating a congregation of 6,000 was built for him in 1861. In 1887 he failed to persuade the Baptist Union to adopt a credal basis as a means of stemming the 'Downgrade' which he saw in the life of the denomination from which he withdrew.

JOHN THOMAS (1821–92): Brought up as a Calvinistic Methodist he became an Independent in 1838. From 1854 onwards he had a notable pastorate in Liverpool but he was accused of trying to introduce a presbyterian polity into Congregationalism.

ROBERT VAUGHAN (1795–1868): Congregational minister, Professor of History, University College, London 1834–43, subsequently president, Lancashire Independent College, Manchester 1843–57, founded the *British Quarterly Review*, a Dissenting journal of considerable literary merit to combat the older *Eclectic Review*'s championship of voluntaryism in education, and as editor (1845–66) made it a vehicle for demonstrating that Nonconformity and culture were not incompatible. Chairman, Congregational Union, 1846.

DATE DUE